Eating Disorders

Series Editor: Cara Acred

Volume 249

Independence Educational Publishers

First published by Independence Educational Publishers

The Studio, High Green

Great Shelford

Cambridge CB22 5EG

England

© Independence 2013

British Library Cataloguing in Publication Data

Eating disorders. -- (Issues ; 249)

1. Eating disorders. 2. Body image disturbance.

I. Series II. Acred, Cara editor of compilation.

616.8'526-dc23

ISBN-13: 9781861686558

Printed in Great Britain

MWL Print Group Ltd

Contents

Introduction

Eating Disorders is Volume 249 in the **ISSUES** series. The aim of the series is to offer current, diverse information about important issues in our world, from a UK perspective.

ABOUT EATING DISORDERS

Recent figures suggest that as many as 1.6 million people in the UK are affected by some form of eating disorder. These disorders range from the more commonly known anorexia and bulimia to the lesser known, but equally as damaging, diabulimia and orthorexia. This book explores the signs, symptoms and effects of eating disorders. It also raises debates surrounding the influence of the media; the morality of pro-ana and pro-mia websites and the disturbing trend of social media fuelled 'thinspiration'. We also consider thought-provoking and challenging issues such as whether anorexic patients should be force-fed when they become severely ill and the morality of the talent scouts who frequent eating disorder clinics looking for potential models.

OUR SOURCES

Titles in the **ISSUES** series are designed to function as educational resource books, providing a balanced overview of a specific subject.

The information in our books is comprised of facts, articles and opinions from many different sources, including:

⇨ Newspaper reports and opinion pieces

⇨ Website factsheets

⇨ Magazine and journal articles

⇨ Statistics and surveys

⇨ Government reports

⇨ Literature from special interest groups

A NOTE ON CRITICAL EVALUATION

Because the information reprinted here is from a number of different sources, readers should bear in mind the origin of the text and whether the source is likely to have a particular bias when presenting information (or when conducting their research). It is hoped that, as you read about the many aspects of the issues explored in this book, you will critically evaluate the information presented.

It is important that you decide whether you are being presented with facts or opinions. Does the writer give a biased or unbiased report? If an opinion is being expressed, do you agree with the writer? Is there potential bias to the 'facts' or statistics behind an article?

ASSIGNMENTS

In the back of this book, you will find a selection of assignments designed to help you engage with the articles you have been reading and to explore your own opinions. Some tasks will take longer than others and there is a mixture of design, writing and research based activities that you can complete alone or in a group.

FURTHER RESEARCH

At the end of each article we have listed its source and a website that you can visit if you would like to conduct your own research. Please remember to critically evaluate any sources that you consult and consider whether the information you are viewing is accurate and unbiased.

Useful weblinks

www.anred.com

www.b-eat.co.uk

www.boyanorexia.com

www.careukeatingdisorders.com

www.eating-disorders.org.uk

www.eatingdisordersadvice.co.uk

www.familylives.org.uk

www.malehealth.co.uk

www.mind.org.uk

www.nedc.com.au

www.nightingalehospital.co.uk

Eating disorders: information and advice

Information from Capio Nightingale Hospital.

We hope that this article will be helpful if:

⇨ You feel that your eating or dieting may be a problem.

⇨ You think you might have anorexia or bulimia.

⇨ Other people worry that you have lost too much weight.

⇨ You have a friend or relative, son or daughter, who is having a problem of this sort.

It does not deal with the problems of being overweight.

We all have different eating habits. There are a large number of 'eating styles' which can allow us to stay healthy. However, there are some which are driven by an intense fear of becoming fat and which actually damage our health. These are called 'eating disorders' and involve:

⇨ Eating too much.

⇨ Eating too little.

⇨ Using harmful ways to get rid of calories.

This article deals with two eating disorders – anorexia nervosa and bulimia nervosa. It describes the two disorders separately:

⇨ The symptoms of anorexia and bulimia are often mixed – some people say that they have 'bulimarexia'.

⇨ The pattern of symptoms can change over time – you may start with anorexic symptoms, but later develop the symptoms of bulimia.

Who gets eating disorders?

Girls and women are ten times more likely than boys and men to suffer from anorexia or bulimia. However, eating disorders do seem to be getting more common in boys and men. They occur more often in people who have been overweight as children.

Anorexia nervosa

What are the signs?

You find that you:

⇨ Worry more and more about your weight.

⇨ Eat less and less.

⇨ Exercise more and more, to burn off calories.

⇨ Can't stop losing weight, even when you are well below a safe weight for your age and height.

⇨ Smoke more or chew gum to keep your weight down.

⇨ Lose interest in sex.

⇨ In girls or women – monthly menstrual periods become irregular or stop.

⇨ In men or boys – erections and wet dreams stop, testicles shrink.

When does it start?

Usually in the teenage years. It affects around:

⇨ One 15-year-old girl in every 150.

⇨ One 15-year-old boy in every 1,000.

⇨ It can also start in childhood or in later life.

What happens?

⇨ You take in very few calories every day. You eat 'healthily' – fruit, vegetables and salads – but they don't give your body enough energy.

⇨ You may also exercise, use slimming pills, or smoke more to keep your weight down.

⇨ You don't want to eat yourself, but you buy food and cook for other people.

⇨ You still get as hungry as ever, in fact you can't stop thinking about food.

⇨ You become more afraid of putting on weight, and more determined to keep your weight well below normal.

⇨ Your family may be the first to notice your thinness and weight loss.

⇨ You may find yourself lying to other people about the amount you are eating and how much weight you are losing.

⇨ You may also develop some of the symptoms of bulimia. Unlike someone with bulimia nervosa, your weight may continue to be very low.

Bulimia nervosa

What are the signs?

You find that you:

⇨ Worry more and more about your weight.

⇨ Binge eat.

⇨ Make yourself vomit and/or use laxatives to get rid of calories.

⇨ Have irregular menstrual periods.

⇨ Feel tired.

⇨ Feel guilty.

⇨ Stay a normal weight, in spite of your efforts to diet.

When does it start?

Bulimia nervosa often starts in the mid-teens. However, people don't usually seek help for it until their early to mid-twenties because they are able to hide it, even though it affects their work and social life.

People most often seek help when their life changes – the start of a new relationship or having to live with other people for the first time.

About four out of every 100 women suffers from bulimia at some time in their lives, rather fewer men.

Bingeing

You raid the fridge or go out and buy lots of fattening foods that you would normally avoid. You then go back to your room, or home, and eat it all, quickly, in secret. You might get through packets of biscuits, several boxes of chocolates and a number of cakes in just a couple of hours. You may even take someone else's food, or shoplift, to satisfy the urge to binge.

Afterwards you feel stuffed and bloated – and probably guilty and depressed. You try to get rid of the food you have eaten by making yourself sick, or by purging with laxatives. It is very uncomfortable and tiring, but you find yourself trapped in a routine of binge eating, and vomiting and/or purging.

Binge eating disorder

This is a pattern of behaviour that has recently been recognised.

It involves dieting and binge eating, but not vomiting. It is distressing, but much less harmful than bulimia. Sufferers are more likely to become overweight.

How can anorexia and bulimia affect you?

Psychological symptoms

⇨ Sleep badly.

⇨ Find it difficult to concentrate or think clearly about anything other than food or calories.

⇨ Feel depressed.

⇨ Lose interest in other people.

⇨ Become obsessive about food and eating (and sometimes other things such as washing, cleaning or tidiness).

Physical symptoms

⇨ Find it harder to eat because your stomach has shrunk.

⇨ Feel tired, weak and cold as your body's metabolism slows down.

⇨ Become constipated.

⇨ Not grow to your full height.

⇨ Get brittle bones which break easily.

⇨ Be unable to get pregnant.

⇨ Damage your liver, particularly if you drink alcohol.

⇨ In extreme cases, you may die. Anorexia nervosa has the highest death rate of any psychological disorder.

If you vomit, you may:

⇨ Lose the enamel on your teeth (it is dissolved by the stomach acid in your vomit).

⇨ Get a puffy face (the salivary glands in your cheeks swell up).

⇨ Notice your heart beating irregularly – palpitations (vomiting disturbs the balance of salts in your blood).

⇨ Feel weak.

⇨ Feel tired all the time.

⇨ Damage your kidneys.

⇨ Have epileptic fits.

⇨ Be unable to get pregnant.

If you use laxatives regularly, you may:

⇨ Have persistent stomach pain.

⇨ Get swollen fingers.

⇨ Find that you can't go to the toilet any more without using laxatives (using laxatives all the time can damage the muscles in your bowel).

⇨ Have huge weight swings. You lose lots of fluid when you purge, but take it all in again when you drink water

afterwards (no calories are lost using laxatives).

What causes eating disorders?

There is no simple answer, but these ideas have all been suggested as explanations:

Social pressure

Our social surroundings powerfully influence our behaviour. Societies which don't value thinness have fewer eating disorders. Places where thinness is valued, such as ballet schools, have more eating disorders.

'Thin is beautiful' in Western culture. Television, newspapers and magazines show pictures of idealised, artificially slim people. So, at some time or other, most of us try to diet. Some of us diet too much, and slip into anorexia.

Lack of an 'off' switch

Most of us can only diet so much before our body tells us that it is time to start eating again. Some people with anorexia may not have this same body 'switch' and can keep their body weight dangerously low for a long time.

Control

It can be very satisfying to diet. Most of us know the feeling of achievement when the scales tell us that we have lost a couple of pounds. It is good to feel that we can control ourselves in a clear, visible way. It may be that your weight is the only part of your life over which you feel you do have any control.

Puberty

Anorexia can reverse some of the physical changes of becoming an adult – pubic and facial hair in men, breasts and menstrual periods in women. This may help to put off the demands of getting older, particularly sexual ones.

Family

Eating is an important part of our lives with other people. Accepting food gives pleasure and refusing it will often upset someone. This is particularly true within families. Saying 'no' to food may be the only way you can express your feelings, or have any say in family affairs.

Depression

Most of us have eaten for comfort when we have been upset, or even just bored. People with bulimia are often depressed, and it may be that binges start off as a way of coping with feelings of unhappiness. Unfortunately, vomiting and using laxatives can leave you feeling just as bad.

Low self-esteem

People with anorexia and bulimia often don't think much of themselves, and compare themselves unfavourably to other people. Losing weight can be a way of trying to get a sense of respect and self-worth.

Emotional distress

We all react differently when bad things happen, or when our lives change. Anorexia and bulimia have been related to:

⇨ Life difficulties.

⇨ Sexual abuse.

⇨ Physical illness.

⇨ Upsetting events – a death or the break-up of a relationship.

⇨ Important events – marriage or leaving home.

The vicious circle

An eating disorder can continue even when the original stress or reason for it has passed. Once your stomach has shrunk, it can feel uncomfortable and frightening to eat.

Physical causes

Some doctors think that there may be a physical cause that we don't yet understand.

Is it different for men?

⇨ Eating disorders do seem to have become more common in boys and men.

⇨ Eating disorders are more common in occupations which demand a low body weight (or low body fat). These include body building, wrestling, dancing, swimming and athletics.

⇨ It may be that men are now seeking help for eating disorders rather than keeping quiet about them.

People with special needs and younger children

A learning difficulty, autism or some other developmental problems can disrupt eating. For example, some people with autism may take a dislike to the colour or texture of foods, and refuse to eat them. The eating problems of pre-teen children are more to do with food texture, 'picky eating' or being angry rather than with wanting to be very thin. The ways of helping these problems are rather different from those for anorexia and bulimia.

Do I have a problem?

A questionnaire used by doctors asks:

⇨ Do you make yourself sick because you're uncomfortably full?

⇨ Do you worry that you've lost control over how much you eat?

⇨ Have you recently lost more than six kilograms (about a stone) in three months?

⇨ Do you believe you're fat when others say you're thin?

⇨ Would you say that food dominates your life?

If you answer 'yes' to two or more of these questions, you may have a problem with your eating.

Helping yourself

⇨ Bulimia can sometimes be tackled using a self-help manual with some guidance from a therapist.

⇨ Anorexia usually needs more organised help from a clinic or therapist. It is still worth getting as much information as you can about the options, so that you can make the best choices for yourself.

Do:

⇨ Stick to regular mealtimes – breakfast, lunch and dinner. If your weight is very low, have morning, afternoon and night-time snacks.

⇨ Try to think of one small step you could take towards a healthier way of eating. If you can't face eating breakfast, try sitting at the table for a few minutes at breakfast time and just drinking a glass of water. When you have got used to doing this, have just a little to eat, even half a slice of toast – but do it every day.

⇨ Keep a diary of what you eat, when you eat it and what your thoughts and feelings have been every day. You can use this to see if there are connections between how you feel, what you are thinking about, and how you eat.

⇨ Try to be honest about what you are or are not eating, both with yourself and with other people.

⇨ Remind yourself that you don't always have to be achieving things – let yourself off the hook sometimes.

⇨ Remind yourself that, if you lose more weight, you will feel more anxious and depressed.

⇨ Make two lists – one of what your eating disorder has given you, one of what you have lost through it. A self-help book can help you with this.

⇨ Try to be kind to your body, don't punish it.

⇨ Make sure you know what a reasonable weight is for you, and that you understand why.

⇨ Read stories of other people's experiences of recovery. You can find these in self-help books or on the Internet.

⇨ Think about joining a self-help group. Your GP may be able to recommend one, or you can contact the Eating Disorders Association.

Don't:

⇨ Weigh yourself more than once a week.

⇨ Spend time checking your body and looking at yourself in the mirror. Nobody is perfect. The longer you look at yourself, the more likely you are to find something you don't like.

Constant checking can make the most attractive person unhappy with the way they look.

⇨ Cut yourself off from family and friends. You may want to because they think you are too thin, but they can be a lifeline.

Avoid websites that encourage you to lose weight and stay at a very low body weight. They encourage you to damage your health, but won't do anything to help when you fall ill.

What if I don't have any help or don't change my eating habits?

Most people with a serious eating disorder will end up having some sort of treatment, so it is not clear what will happen if nothing is done. However, it looks as though most serious eating disorders don't get better on their own. Some sufferers from anorexia will die – this is less likely to happen if you do not vomit, do not use laxatives and do not drink alcohol.

Professional help

⇨ Your GP can refer you to a specialist counsellor, psychiatrist or psychologist.

⇨ You may choose a private therapist, self-help group or clinic, but it is still safer to let your GP know what is happening.

⇨ It's wise to have a good physical health check. Your eating disorder may have caused physical problems. Less commonly, you may have an unrecognised medical condition.

⇨ The most helpful treatments for you will probably depend on your particular symptoms, your age and situation.

⇨ The above information is reprinted with kind permission from Capio Nightingale Hospital. Please visit www.nightingalehospital.co.uk for further information.

Facts and figures

How many people in the UK have an eating disorder?

There is a lack of data detailing how many people in the UK suffer from an eating disorder. Although the Department of Health provides hospital episode statistics, these only include those affected by eating disorders who are in inpatient NHS treatment. These figures therefore leave out all those who have not come forward, have not been diagnosed, are receiving private treatment, or are being treated as an outpatient or in the community. We continue to request that the Department of Health conducts reliable studies to provide us with these vital statistics.

The most accurate figures we are aware of are those from the National Institute of Health and Clinical Excellence. These suggest that 1.6 million people in the UK are affected by an eating disorder, of which around 11% are male. However, more recent research from the NHS information centre showed that up to 6.4% of adults displayed signs of an eating disorder (Adult Psychiatric Morbidity Survey, 2007). This survey also showed that a quarter of those showing signs of an eating disorder were male, a figure much higher than previous studies had suggested.

It is estimated that of those with eating disorders:

⇨ 10% of sufferers are anorexic,

⇨ 40% are bulimic, and

⇨ the rest fall into the EDNOS category, including those with binge eating disorder.

The hospital episode statistics do give an indication of regional figures, and differences between sexes and age-ranges, but as explained above these statistics only describe a small part of the problem.

At what age do people develop eating disorders?

Although many eating disorders develop during adolescence, it is not at all unusual for people to develop eating disorders earlier or later in life. In fact, we are aware of cases of anorexia nervosa in children as young as six, and some research reports cases developing in women in their 70s. What we do know is that outside of the stereotypical age bracket, people are less likely to be appropriately diagnosed due to a lack of understanding and awareness of eating disorders in these age groups.

Can men get eating disorders?

Yes. Reports vary, but many estimate that males make up anywhere from 10% to a quarter of sufferers. As with older and younger patients, males with eating disorders may be less likely to be diagnosed due to a lack

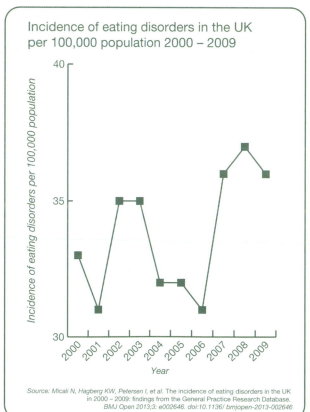

Incidence of eating disorders in the UK per 100,000 population 2000 – 2009

Incidence of eating disorders per 100,000 population

Year

Source: Micali N, Hagberg KW, Petersen I, et al. The incidence of eating disorders in the UK in 2000 – 2009: findings from the General Practice Research Database. BMJ Open 2013;3: e002646. doi:10.1136/ bmjopen-2013-002646

of awareness, or may be less likely to come forward due to a perceived stigma attached to eating disorders in general and specifically to men with eating disorders.

What is the average duration of an eating disorder?

Due to a lack of sufficient evidence, it is difficult to say exactly how long eating disorders last for on average. Research carried out in Australia suggests that the average duration of anorexia nervosa is eight years, and of bulimia nervosa five years. However, we also know from research into severe and enduring eating disorders that these illnesses can last for many years, having a debilitating effect on the sufferers and their families. The research suggests that the earlier treatment is sought, the better the sufferer's chance of recovery.

Is it possible to recover from an eating disorder?

Yes. We are lucky enough to work with some very inspirational people, and we have heard some very uplifting stories of recovery. Reviews of the research into recovery suggest that around 46% of anorexia nervosa patients fully recover, with a third improving, and 20% remaining chronically ill. Similar research into bulimia suggests that around 45% of sufferers make a full recovery, 27% improve considerably, and 23% suffer chronically. We are not aware of any studies that examine recovery rates in binge-eating disorder. Our view is that eating disorders can and will be beaten.

How devastating are eating disorders?

Anorexia has the highest mortality rate of any psychiatric disorder, from medical complications associated with the illness as well as suicide. Research has found that 20% of anorexia sufferers will die prematurely from their illness. Bulimia is also associated with severe medical complications, and binge eating disorder sufferers often experience the medical complications associated with obesity. In every case, eating disorders severely affect the quality

of life of the sufferer and those that care for them.

How should eating disorder sufferers seek help?

The first port of call for a sufferer should always be their GP. The Beat helplines are available for support and information, and can give people suggestions for how to approach their doctor. The care pathway for patients with eating disorders is outlined here: http://healthguides. mapofmedicine.com/choices/map/ eating_disorders1.html.

Do eating disorders run in families?

Multiple factors contribute to the development of an eating disorder, but research suggests that genetics do play a role in this. Some research has found that female relatives of anorexia sufferers were 11.4 times more likely to suffer from anorexia compared to relatives of unaffected participants. For female relatives of those with bulimia, the likelihood of developing bulimia was 3.7 times that of those with unaffected relatives. This and other research does suggest a link between family members, although it is not yet totally clear how much of this influence is genetic and how much is due to environmental factors. What we do know is that many other factors also affect the development of an eating disorder.

How can you tell if someone has an eating disorder?

You cannot tell if someone has an eating disorder just by looking at them. While it is true that some sufferers of anorexia are severely emaciated, some are not, and the majority of eating disorder sufferers do not have anorexia. Those suffering from bulimia may be within the normal weight range or may be overweight, while those with binge eating disorder are often overweight.

Eating disorders can only be diagnosed by a clinician. However, the SCOFF screening tool, developed by Professor John Morgan at Leeds and York Partnerships NHS Foundation Trust, can indicate a possible eating disorder. A score of two or more positive answers

is a positive screen for an eating disorder.

What is a healthy weight?

A healthy weight will depend on the age and height of an individual. The diagnostic criteria for anorexia nervosa include the refusal to maintain, or to reach, 85% of the expected body weight for someone of that age and height. Sometimes people refer to body mass index (BMI) to assess whether someone is of a healthy weight. Specific BMI charts can also be referred to, to determine whether an individual's BMI is healthy for their age and height. In general, a BMI below 17.5 is seen as indicative of anorexia nervosa, whereas the ideal BMI is anywhere between 18.5 and 24.9, and those over a BMI of 25 are classed as overweight.

Where can I find out more?

You may find the following links useful:

National Institute of Health and Clinical Excellence (NICE) guidelines:

http://www.nice.org.uk/nicemedia/ live/10932/29220/29220.pdf

Institute of Psychiatry Eating Disorders Research page:

http://www.iop.kcl.ac.uk/sites/ edu/?id=131

Adult Psychiatric Morbidity Survey (2007):

http://www.ic.nhs.uk/pubs/ psychiatricmorbidity07

For information on Pica:

http://www.thecbf.org.uk/

⇨ The above information is reprinted with kind permission from Beat, the national eating disorders charity. Please visit www.b-eat.co.uk for further information.

Types of eating disorders

The better known eating disorders

There are many diseases, disorders, and problem conditions involving food, eating and weight, but in everyday conversation the term 'eating disorders' has come to mean anorexia nervosa, bulimia and binge eating, which are defined on this page. Definitions of lesser-known problems, are on the next page.

Anorexia nervosa: the relentless pursuit of thinness

⇨ Person refuses to maintain normal body weight for age and height.

⇨ Weighs 85% or less than what is expected for age and height.

⇨ In women, menstrual periods stop. In men, levels of sex hormones fall.

⇨ Young girls do not begin to menstruate at the appropriate age.

⇨ Person denies the dangers of low weight.

⇨ Is terrified of becoming fat.

⇨ Is terrified of gaining weight even though s/he is markedly underweight.

⇨ Reports feeling fat even when very thin.

In addition, anorexia nervosa often includes depression, irritability, withdrawal, and peculiar behaviours such as compulsive rituals, strange eating habits, and division of foods into 'good/safe' and 'bad/dangerous' categories. Person may have low tolerance for change and new situations; may fear growing up and assuming adult responsibilities and an adult lifestyle. May be overly engaged with or dependent on parents or family. Dieting may represent avoidance of, or ineffective attempts to cope with, the demands of a new life stage such as adolescence.

Bulimia nervosa: the diet-binge-purge disorder

⇨ Person binge eats.

⇨ Feels out of control while eating.

⇨ Vomits, misuses laxatives, exercises or fasts to get rid of the calories.

⇨ Diets when not bingeing. Becomes hungry and binges again.

⇨ Believes self-worth requires being thin. (It does not.)

⇨ May shoplift, be promiscuous, and abuse alcohol, drugs and credit cards.

⇨ Weight may be normal or near normal unless anorexia is also present.

Like anorexia, bulimia can kill. Even though bulimics put up a brave front, they are often depressed, lonely, ashamed and empty inside. Friends may describe them as competent and fun to be with, but underneath, where they hide their guilty secrets, they are hurting. Feeling unworthy, they have great difficulty talking about their feelings, which almost always include anxiety, depression, self-doubt and deeply buried anger. Impulse control may be a problem; e.g. shoplifting, sexual adventurousness, alcohol and drug abuse, and other kinds of risk-taking behaviour. Person acts with little consideration of consequences.

Binge eating disorder

⇨ The person binge eats frequently and repeatedly.

⇨ Feels out of control and unable to stop eating during binges.

⇨ May eat rapidly and secretly, or may snack and nibble all day long.

⇨ Feels guilty and ashamed of binge eating.

⇨ Has a history of diet failures.

⇨ Tends to be depressed and obese.

People who have binge eating disorder do not regularly vomit, overexercise or abuse laxatives like bulimics do. They may be genetically predisposed to weigh more than the cultural ideal (which at present is exceedingly unrealistic), so they diet, make themselves hungry, and then binge in response to that hunger. Or they may eat for emotional reasons: to comfort themselves, avoid threatening situations and numb emotional pain. Regardless of the reason, diet programmes are not the answer. In fact, diets almost always make matters worse. Information reported in the March 2002 *New England Journal of Medicine* suggests that for some, but not all, people a genetic flaw in combination with lifestyle factors can predispose to binge eating and subsequent obesity.

Eating disorders not otherwise specified (EDNOS)

⇨ An official diagnosis. The phrase describes atypical eating disorders.

⇨ Including situations in which a person meets all but a few of the criteria for a particular diagnosis.

⇨ What the person is doing with regard to food and weight is neither normal nor healthy.

Less-well-known eating disorders and related problems

⇨ There are many diseases, disorders, and problem conditions involving food, eating and weight. Here are brief descriptions of problems other than anorexia nervosa, bulimia and binge eating disorder.

Anorexia athletica (compulsive exercising)

⇨ Not a formal diagnosis. The behaviours are usually a part of anorexia nervosa, bulimia or obsessive-compulsive disorder.

⇨ The person repeatedly exercises beyond the requirements for good health.

⇨ May be a fanatic about weight and diet.

⇨ Steals time to exercise from work, school and relationships.

⇨ Focuses on challenge. Forgets that physical activity can be fun.

⇨ Defines self-worth in terms of performance.

⇨ Is rarely or never satisfied with athletic achievements.

⇨ Does not savour victory. Pushes on to the next challenge immediately.

⇨ Justifies excessive behaviour by defining self as a 'special' elite athlete.

⇨ Compulsive exercising is not an official diagnosis as are anorexia, bulimia and binge eating disorder. We include it here because many people who are preoccupied with food and weight exercise compulsively in attempts to control weight. The real issues are not weight and performance excellence but rather control and self-respect.

Body dysmorphic disorder (BDD)

⇨ BDD is thought to be a sub-type of obsessive-compulsive disorder. It is not a variant of anorexia nervosa or bulimia nervosa.

⇨ The person with an eating disorder says, 'I am so fat.' The person with BDD says, 'I am so ugly.'

⇨ BDD often includes social phobias. Sufferers are shy and withdrawn in new situations and with unfamiliar people.

⇨ BDD affects about two per cent of the people in the United States. It strikes males and females equally. 70 percent of cases appear before age 18.

⇨ Sufferers are excessively concerned about appearance, in particular perceived flaws of face, hair and skin. They are convinced these flaws exist in spite of reassurances from friends and family members who usually can see nothing to justify such intense worry and anxiety.

⇨ BDD sufferers are at elevated risk for despair and suicide. In some cases they undergo multiple, unnecessary plastic surgeries.

⇨ BDD is treatable and begins with an evaluation by a physician and mental health care provider.

Treatments thus far found to be effective include medication (especially meds that adjust serotonin levels in the brain) and cognitive-behavioural therapy. A clinician makes the diagnosis and recommends treatment based on the needs and circumstances of each person.

Muscle dysmorphic disorder (bigorexia)

⇨ A subtype of body dysmorphic disorder, described above.

⇨ Sometimes called bigorexia, muscle dysmorphia is the opposite of anorexia nervosa. People with this disorder obsess about being small and undeveloped. They worry that they are too little and too frail. Even if they have good muscle mass, they believe their muscles are inadequate.

Infection-triggered, auto-immune subtype of anorexia nervosa in young children

⇨ Not an official eating disorder, but the topic has gathered the interest of researchers.

⇨ May be related to a type of obsessive-compulsive disorder triggered by an autoimmune process involving bacteria or viruses and parts of the nervous system.

⇨ May be related to paediatric infection-triggered autoimmune neuropsychiatric disorders (PITANDS) and paediatric autoimmune neuropsychiatric disorders associated with streptococcus (PANDAS)

⇨ Suspected when symptoms and behaviours typical of anorexia nervosa appear suddenly in a young child, or when symptoms and behaviours in a young child worsen quickly with no other explanation

⇨ And when the child has had a recent respiratory, throat or other infection.

⇨ Antibiotics, antivirals and/or vaccines may be part of the treatment, either after refusal to eat appears or as prevention.

- The first step in treatment is a thorough evaluation done by a paediatrician who is familiar with PITANDS and PANDAS research.

- Reference for physicians: *Journal of the American Academy of Child and Adolescent Psychiatry*, Volume 36, Number 8.

Orthorexia nervosa

- Not an official eating disorder diagnosis, but the concept is useful. The name was coined by Steven Bratman, M.D. to describe 'a pathological fixation on eating "proper" or "pure" or "superior" food'.

- People with orthorexia nervosa feel superior to others who eat 'improper' food, which might include non-organic or junk foods and items found in regular grocery stores, as opposed to health food stores.

- Orthorexics obsess over what to eat, how much to eat, how to prepare food 'properly,' and where to obtain 'pure' and 'proper' foods.

- Eating the 'right' food becomes an important, or even the primary, focus of life. One's worth or goodness is seen in terms of what one does or does not eat. Personal values, relationships, career goals and friendships become less important than the quality and timing of what is consumed.

- Perhaps related to, or a type of, obsessive-compulsive disorder.

Night-eating syndrome

- The person has little or no appetite for breakfast. Delays first meal for several hours after waking up. Is often upset about how much was eaten the night before.

- Most of the day's calories are eaten late in the day or at night.

Nocturnal sleep-related eating disorder

- Thought to be a sleep disorder, not an eating disorder.

- Person sleep eats and may sleep walk as well.

Rumination syndrome

- Person eats, swallows and then regurgitates food back into the mouth where it is chewed and swallowed again. Process may be repeated several times or for several hours per episode.

- Rumination may be voluntary or involuntary.

- Ruminators report that regurgitated material does not taste bitter, and that it is returned to the mouth with a gentle burp, not violent gagging or retching – not even nausea.

Gourmand syndrome

- Person is preoccupied with fine food, including its purchase, preparation, presentation and consumption.

- Exceedingly rare; thought to be caused by injury to the brain.

Prader-Willi syndrome

- A congenital problem usually associated with mental retardation and behaviour problems, including a drive to eat constantly that will not be denied.

Pica

- A craving for non-food items such as dirt, clay, plaster, chalk or paint chips.

- Cyclic vomiting syndrome.

- Cycles of frequent vomiting, usually (but not always) found in children.

- May be related to, or share neurological mechanisms with, migraine headaches.

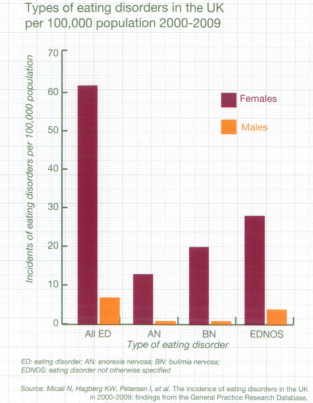

Types of eating disorders in the UK per 100,000 population 2000-2009

ED: eating disorder; AN: anorexia nervosa; BN: bulimia nervosa; EDNOS: eating disorder not otherwise specified

Source: Micali N, Hagberg KW, Petersen I, et al. The incidence of eating disorders in the UK in 2000-2009: findings from the General Practice Research Database. BMJ Open 2013;3: e002646. doi:10.1136/ bmjopen-2013-002646

Chewing and spitting

- The person puts food in his/her mouth, tastes it, chews it and then spits it out.

- Some people think this is a separate eating disorder. It is not. It is a calorie-control behaviour commonly seen in anorexia nervosa, and sometimes in bulimia and eating-disorder-not-otherwise-specified. The person is creative, allowing some experience and enjoyment of food but avoiding calories. Since essential nutrients are not incorporated into the body, chewing and spitting can be just as harmful to health as are starvation dieting and binge eating followed by purging.

- The above information is reprinted with kind permission from ANRED. Please visit www.anred.com for further information.

The staggering cost of eating disorders in England

A newly released report carried out for Beat by a volunteer economist from the charity Pro Bono Economics (PBE) has found an overall estimated cost of £1.26 billion per year to the English economy from eating disorders – and could be much higher.

The report sought to form a comprehensive view of the overall costs to society of eating disorders in England, especially amongst young people, and the costs to the NHS, employers and employees.

The report, by economist John Henderson volunteering with PBE, reveals overall healthcare costs estimated at £80-£100 million, costs of reduced GDP up to £2.9 billion, and costs of reduced length of life and health up to £6.6 billion.

With mental ill health representing up to 23% of the total burden of ill health in the UK, and estimated to double over the next 20 years, the findings of the report demonstrate the severity of the impact of eating disorders on society at large.

Beat has long campaigned for early intervention – 'Eating disorders have the highest mortality rate of all mental health disorders,' said Chief Executive Susan Ringwood. 'It is vital that the individual is able to access the right specialist treatment as early as possible. Young lives are being disrupted at crucial stages in their development with loss of education, hindering career prospects and premature death. This report clearly demonstrates that healthcare costs would be better spent earlier to stop the effects on sufferers, their family and the community.'

Sue Holloway, Pro Bono Economics Director, says: 'This is the first serious attempt to quantify comprehensively the costs of eating disorders in England and the resulting estimate shows the significant scale of the problem. We hope this will support Beat to achieve its vision that eating disorders can be beaten.'

22-year-old Francesca from Berkshire finds herself having to repay an extra year's student loan for tuition fees when she was too ill to attend university. 'I have suffered for eight years and it's affected me in a lot of ways. I was told for numerous years that I was not ill enough for treatment until eventually I became so ill that my parents paid for me to attend a private unit. The NHS waiting list was too long. I've had state-funded therapy for two years. My education has been adversely affected over the years and I have also suffered numerous

physical health problems as a result of my eating disorder. I truly believe that if I had been given treatment earlier, my problems would not have escalated and I would not have needed so much help later on – at a cost to my family and the state.'

23-year-old Annabelle from London was also told that her eating disorder was not severe enough for treatment. 'By the time I received help I was in hospital for 18 months, missing almost two years of education and had to drop half my GCSEs. I also had a relapse during university and had to take a year out when my internal organs began failing. I have osteoporosis as a result of my illness.'

And males face similar problems with the added exacerbation that through ignorance and misunderstanding, their illness is not readily recognised. 'I went for years and years without knowing where to turn, or not taken seriously when I did ask,' says 42-year-old David from London. 'It was only when I'd caused major damage to my body and mind that things were noticed. My life would be very different if I'd received treatment at the outset.'

Visit www.b-eat.co.uk to download the full report *Costs of eating disorders in England: economic impact of anorexia nervosa, bulimia nervosa and other disorders focussing on young people.*

31 January 2012

⇨ The above information is reprinted with kind permission from Beat. Please visit www. b-eat.co.uk. For further information and additional case studies, please contact Mary George, Press Officer, on 0300 123 7061 or email media@ b-eat.co.uk

Disordered eating

Disordered eating is when a person regularly engages in destructive eating behaviours such as restrictive dieting, compulsive eating or skipping meals. Disordered eating can include behaviours which reflect many but not all of the symptoms of eating disorders such as anorexia nervosa, bulimia nervosa, binge eating disorder or eating disorder not otherwise specified (EDNOS).

Disordered eating and dieting behaviour are the most common indicators of the development of an eating disorder. Eating disorders are severe and life-threatening mental illnesses. An eating disorder is not a lifestyle choice.

Disordered eating can have a destructive impact upon a person's life and has been linked to a reduced ability to cope with stressful situations. There is also increased incidence of suicidal thoughts and behaviours in adolescents with disordered eating.

Examples of disordered eating include:

⇨ Fasting or chronic restrained eating.

⇨ Skipping meals.

⇨ Binge eating.

⇨ Self-induced vomiting.

⇨ Restrictive dieting.

⇨ Unbalanced eating (e.g. restricting a major food group such as 'fatty' foods or carbohydrates).

⇨ Laxative, diuretic, enema misuse.

⇨ Steroid and creatine use – supplements designed to enhance athletic performance and alter physical appearance.

⇨ Using diet pills.

Why are disordered eating and dieting dangerous?

Not everyone who diets will develop an eating disorder but it would be hard to find a person with an eating disorder who has not been on a diet themselves. Dieting is one of the most common forms of disordered eating.

Severely restricting the amount of food you eat can be a very dangerous practice. When the body is starved of food it responds by reducing the rate at which it burns energy (the metabolic rate), this can result in overeating and binge eating behaviours that can lead to weight gain and obesity.

Feelings of guilt and failure are common in people who engage in disordered eating. These feelings can arise as a result of binge eating, 'breaking' a diet or weight gain. A person with disordered eating behaviours may isolate themselves for fear of socialising in situations where people will be eating. This can contribute to low self-esteem and significant emotional impairment.

Diets don't work

95 per cent of people who diet will return to their usual weight, or weigh even more, within two years. Weight loss and 'fad' diets do not take individual requirements into consideration and can result in a person feeling hungry, experiencing low moods, lacking in energy levels and developing poor health.

What are the risks associated with disordered eating and dieting?

The risks associated with disordered eating are severe. People with disordered eating may experience:

⇨ A clinical eating disorder (anorexia nervosa, bulimia nervosa, binge eating disorder or eating disorder otherwise not specified).

⇨ Weight gain.

⇨ Osteoporosis – a condition that can lead to human bones becoming fragile and easy to fracture.

⇨ Fatigue and poor sleep quality.

⇨ Constipation and/or diarrhoea.

⇨ Headaches.

⇨ Muscle cramps.

Is it possible to change disordered eating and dieting behaviour?

Yes. It is possible to change eating behaviour, even if you have been engaging in disordered eating and dieting for many years. With the right support and treatment and a high level of personal commitment, your body can learn to function to its full capacity again.

Seeking help from a practitioner with specialised knowledge in health and nutrition can assist you in reversing the adverse effects of disordered eating and restoring emotional, mental and physical health.

Getting help

Disordered eating is the number one cause of the onset of an eating disorder and seeking help early is the best preventative measure. While your GP may not be a specialist in eating disorders, they are a good 'first base'. A GP can provide a referral to a practitioner with specialised knowledge in health, nutrition and eating disorders.

⇨ The above information is from the National Eating Disorders Collaboration article *What is disordered eating?* and is used by permission of the Australian Government. Please visit www.nedc.com.au for further information.

© National Eating Disorders Collaboration 2013

The growing problem of diabulimia

Most people refer to anorexia or bulimia when they talk about eating disorders. However, there is one eating disorder which people know little about – diabulimia. As part of Eating Disorders Awareness Week we looked at this condition and what we are doing at SLaM to treat it.

Imagine being a teenage diabetic and having to inject insulin every meal time, sometimes at school. Not only does that make you different from your peers but it is a demanding and intrusive activity to have to do every day. And if you don't do it, you may die.

But then imagine you can stop doing that – by limiting insulin levels you can avoid those embarrassing injection times and lose weight at the same time. This can lead to a potentially fatal eating disorder called diabulimia.

Many people will never have heard of diabulimia. It is an extremely debilitating condition and one where there is still a massive amount of misunderstanding, even within some parts of the medical profession.

The term has been used to describe people with Type 1 diabetes with bulimia nervosa who use insulin omission as a form of weight control.

Some people develop symptoms of anorexia nervosa and this also has an impact on diabetic control. The nutritional consequences of starvation on the brain and body are very severe when limiting glucose and insulin.

Janet Treasure, Professor of Psychiatry and Director of the Eating Disorder Service at South London and Maudsley NHS Foundation Trust (SLaM), said:

'It is estimated that 40% of Type 1 females aged 15 to 30 years old regularly omit insulin for weight control. The combination of diabetes and an eating disorder produces a serious, pervasive and complex psychiatric condition and should be treated as such, with understanding and compassion but also with urgency as per NICE guidelines.

'Complications include blindness, limb loss, neuropathy blindness and fatality.'

At SLaM we are carrying out pioneering research work to treat people with diabulimia and we are one of the only trusts in the country to specialise in this little-known illness.

SLaM provides care across inpatient, day patient and outpatient sites. Our unit provides a safe healing space where people can explore their difficulties and gain control over their eating disorder, working one-to-one, within a group and as part of their family.

A wide range of evidence-based care packages are available and can be tailored to suit specific needs. The agreed therapeutic aims will vary, but may involve gaining weight and establishing regular eating patterns.

An important part of our work involves family members and carers, helping them come to an understanding of eating disorders, their likely causes and their consequences and also providing support and care in the most effective way. The unit offers an extensive programme of training and consultancy for eating disorder professionals, voluntary workers and teams.

Our unit is internationally renowned for its research and is at the forefront of treatment development, having generated much of the evidence underpinning contemporary eating disorder treatments. The Director of the Eating Disorder Unit, Professor Janet Treasure, has recently been awarded an OBE for services to people with eating disorders.

Treatment for this condition is complex and requires good physical and psychological care. Psychological therapy, which relies on a brain which can learn and reflect, is less effective if brain function is compromised by poor diabetic control. Also, if diabetes professionals ignore emotions around food and body shape then diabetes education will be ineffective.

Signs and symptoms of diabetics with eating disorders (DWED):

⇨ Recurrent episodes of hyperglycaemia.

⇨ Frequent hospitalisations for poor blood sugar control.

⇨ Delay in puberty or sexual maturation or irregular menses/amenorrhoea.

⇨ Frequent trips to the toilet.

⇨ Frequent episodes of thrush/ urine infections.

⇨ Nausea and stomach cramps.

⇨ Loss of appetite/eating more and losing weight.

⇨ Drinking an abnormal amount of fluids.

⇨ Hair loss.

⇨ Delayed healing from infections/ bruises.

Recent research shows that not only are females who have Type 1 diabetes at twice the risk of developing anorexia or bulimia, as many as 40% of 15- to 30-year-olds regularly omit insulin.

SLaM, within Kings Health Partners, provide a unique service for diabetics with eating disorders with psychiatrists in the diabetes teams and eating disorder teams – bridging physical and psychological care. The team at SLaM and KHP are involved in developing and testing new interventions in combination with the charity DWED (Diabetics With Eating Disorders).

13 February 2013

⇨ The above information is reprinted with kind permission from SLaM. Please visit www.slam.nhs.uk for further information.

© SLaM 2013

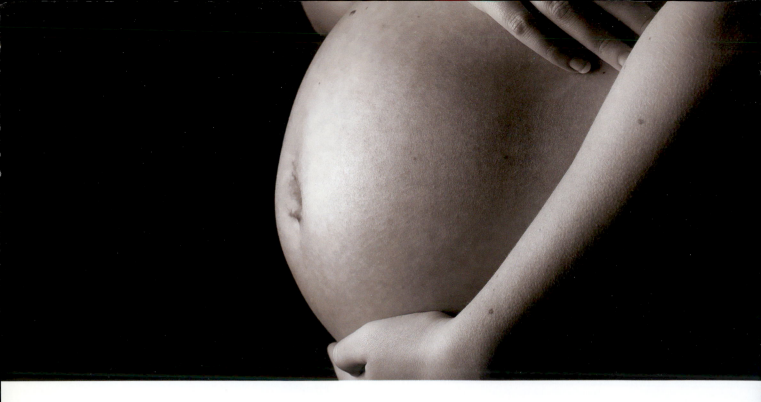

One in 14 women have an eating disorder during pregnancy, research reveals

One in 14 women have an eating disorder in the first three months of their pregnancy, according to research published on Monday.

A survey of more than 700 pregnant women by University College London (UCL) found a quarter were 'highly concerned about their weight and shape'.

Two per cent of those questioned were found to fast, exercise excessively, induce vomiting, and misuse laxatives or diuretics to avoid gaining weight during pregnancy.

The study – funded by the National Institute for Health Research – also found one in 12 pregnant women said they would overeat and lose control over what they ate twice a week.

Dr Nadia Micali, from the UCL Institute of Child Health, who led the study, said: 'There is good evidence from our research that eating disorders in pregnancy can affect both the mother and the developing baby.

'Greater awareness of eating disorders and their symptoms amongst antenatal healthcare professionals would help to better identify and manage such disorders amongst pregnant women.'

The researchers have called for women to be screened for eating disorders at their first antenatal check-up due to the adverse affects on the health of the mother and the baby.

Writing in the *European Eating Disorders Review*, they warned that many pregnant women with eating disorders are currently being left untreated.

Dr Abigail Easter, also from the UCL Institute of Child Health, added: 'Women with eating disorders are often reluctant to disclose their illness to healthcare professionals, possibly due to a fear of stigma or fear that health services might respond in a negative way.

'Typical pregnancy symptoms such as weight gain and vomiting can also mask the presence of an eating disorder. Many women with eating disorders may therefore go undetected and untreated during pregnancy.'

About 1.4 million women nationwide suffer from eating disorders, around 4% of the female population.

The women answered an anonymous questionnaire at their first routine antenatal scan, which asked about their eating habits in the six to 12 months before becoming pregnant.

Any symptoms were assessed during the first three months of their pregnancy.

18 March 2013

⇨ The above information is reprinted with kind permission from *The Huffington Post* (UK). Please visit www.huffingtonpost.co.uk for further information.

What health professionals should know about eating disorders

Key points health professionals should know when dealing with a young person living with and recovering from an eating disorder.

By Ulla Räisänen

Over the course of two years, I have met with 40 young women and men who have shared on film honest details about their experiences of eating disorders. Their hope is that sharing their stories will help other people who are similarly affected to feel less alone and encourage them to seek help.

The research shows that common myths about the illness have prevented many young people from getting the treatment and support they needed, from family, friends and even the health service.

During the course of their eating disorder, young people came into contact with many different types of health professionals including GPs, nurses, counsellors, psychologists, psychiatrists, dieticians, social workers and other support workers.

There are some things that health professionals should know when dealing with a young person living with and recovering from an eating disorder.

Anyone can have an eating disorder

Anyone can become ill with an eating disorder. Eating disorders affect people of all ages, backgrounds, sexualities, both men and women. You can't tell if a person has an eating disorder by just looking at them.

First point of contact is often critical

This first contact with services was often a huge step for a young person. People often found it very difficult to talk about what was going on, trying to hide their problems and it could take months, even years, to seek help. The way they were treated at this point could have a lasting, positive or negative, impact.

Young people hoped that the health professionals would realise just how hard asking for help was and to help nurture and support their confidence to stay in contact with services.

Early intervention is key

Young people often felt that people struggled to recognise the psychological symptoms of eating disorders as well as the range of different eating disorders.

If those who haven't yet developed a full-blown eating disorder could be recognised, they can also be helped earlier. This is critical, as the longer eating disorders are left undiagnosed and untreated, the more serious and harder to treat they can become.

Effective, early intervention could be achieved when health practitioners were knowledgeable, well trained, sensitive and proactive.

Eating disorders are about emotions and behaviours, not just about weight

A common myth that many of the young people had come across was the thought that people with eating disorders were always very underweight. This idea had made it harder for some to get treatment and support or even to be taken seriously by their doctor.

In some cases, young people felt that the only way for them to be taken seriously and be able to access eating disorder services was to lose more weight. This could have serious consequences; the more weight they lost, the harder it was for them to be able to seek or accept help.

See the whole person, not just the eating disorder

Once in contact with health services, above all else, young people wanted not just to be seen 'as an eating disorder' but to be treated as a whole person. It was important that they felt treated as individuals and for health professionals to realise that everyone responded differently.

A good health professional also tried to engage young people on other things than just the eating disorder, hobbies or interests.

Respect the young person

Feeling respected, listened to and being given the space to explain things from their perspective was important for young people during treatment and recovery.

Professionals should take their time and find out what was going on for that particular person, not act on assumptions. Health professionals shouldn't patronise or dismiss issues that were important to the person in front of them.

This research, funded by Comic Relief, has now been published on online at Youthhealthtalk.org.

Ulla Räisänen is a senior researcher with the health experiences research group at University of Oxford, and was responsible for conducting the study published on Youthhealthtalk.org.

12 February 2013

⇨ The above article is reprinted with kind permission from *The Guardian*. Please visit www.guardian.co.uk for further information.

© 2013 Guardian News and Media Limited

The many consequences of anorexia nervosa

People with anorexia are often ambivalent about their recovery. They recognise that their illness addresses very difficult psychological issues and emotions that they do not otherwise know how to cope with. On the other hand, the more insightful will also recognise that the price paid for holding on to their illness is considerable and varied. In this week's blog, a member of our team, Charlotte, gives her insight into just a few of the areas of life that those we care for lose out on.

She writes:

'I was lucky enough this year to take a two-week holiday to America. Although I often go there to see family this time we visited places I have not been to before. For me this was an opportunity to explore, discover, and try new foods and local specialities (guided by my husband's reproduction of a Man vs. Food style restaurant tour). This holiday, like most of my previous holidays, was a mixture of relaxing by the pool, wandering around towns and cities with a very loose plan of where to end up. Basically a spontaneous, unplanned two weeks of indulging cultural, intellectual and culinary appetites.

On reflecting on my enjoyable holiday in America, I took time to think about the trip if a client of mine were to do as I did – one of the Care UK values is that 'We see the world from the point of view of our service users.' The trip I took would be so different to experience as a young person with a severe and enduring eating disorder. Starting the day with no specific plan of what to do, meals out in restaurants where no calories are displayed on the menu, stopping for food when and where the opportunity arose, relaxing on a sun lounger for however long the sun shone for, staying in bed late, and going out for drinks in the evening. I tried to see these holiday 'norms' as a client might experience them. Having accompanied service users on trips and unit holidays, I do know that many of them do not identify with the easy-going description above during these trips. Clients with eating disorders often experience a fear of lacking control, particularly around food. Their eating disorder will not allow them to leave their days unplanned, or eat and drink without cruel and persecutory repercussions. It is so important to not assume that one's own experience is even similar to another's.

I am by no means saying that as a service we should avoid aggravating a client's eating disorder by not challenging their behaviours and rigidity. Encouraging clients to take part in something that their eating disorder does not 'like' or feel comfortable with is essential to treatment. But this must be done with the client's point of view firmly in mind. We cannot only aim to redefine the meaning of the word holiday but the meaning of their life.'

Charlotte's observations illustrate both the negative impact anorexia can have, on what we might consider fundamentals of an ordinary lifestyle, and her thoughtfulness and awareness of this aspect of the disorder. Our teams are well versed in working creatively to help our clients challenge their illness and ultimately to help them to live their life and not their disorder and we hope Charlotte's insight can be helpful to others who are supporting someone with an eating disorder.

5 December 2012

⇨ The above information is reprinted with kind permission from Care UK. Please visit www.careukeatingdisorders.com for further information.

Eating disorders statistics

General:

⇨ Almost 50% of people with eating disorders meet the criteria for depression.[1]

⇨ Only one in ten men and women with eating disorders receive treatment. Only 35% of people that receive treatment for eating disorders get treatment at a specialised facility for eating disorders.[2]

⇨ Up to 24 million people of all ages and genders suffer from an eating disorder (anorexia, bulimia and binge eating disorder) in the U.S.[3]

⇨ Eating disorders have the highest mortality rate of any mental illness.[4]

Students:

⇨ 91% of women surveyed on a college campus had attempted to control their weight through dieting. 22% dieted 'often' or 'always.'[5]

⇨ 86% report onset of eating disorder by age 20; 43% report onset between ages of 16 and 20.[6]

⇨ Anorexia is the third most common chronic illness among adolescents.[7]

⇨ 95% of those who have eating disorders are between the ages of 12 and 25.[8]

⇨ 25% of college-aged women engage in bingeing and purging as a weight-management technique.[3]

⇨ The mortality rate associated with anorexia nervosa is 12 times higher than the death rate associated with all causes of death for females 15 to 24 years old.[4]

⇨ Over one-half of teenage girls and nearly one-third of teenage boys use unhealthy weight control behaviours such as skipping meals, fasting, smoking cigarettes, vomiting and taking laxatives.[17]

⇨ In a survey of 185 female students on a college campus, 58% felt pressure to be a certain weight, and of the 83% that dieted for weight loss, 44% were of normal weight.[16]

Men:

⇨ An estimated ten-15% of people with anorexia or bulimia are male.[9]

⇨ Men are less likely to seek treatment for eating disorders because of the perception that they are 'women's diseases'.[10]

⇨ Among gay men, nearly 14% appeared to suffer from bulimia and over 20% appeared to be anorexic.[11]

Media, perception, dieting:

⇨ 95% of all dieters will regain their lost weight within five years.[3]

⇨ 35% of 'normal dieters' progress to pathological dieting. Of those, 20-25% progress to partial or full-syndrome eating disorders.[5]

⇨ The body type portrayed in advertising as the ideal is possessed naturally by only 5% of American females.[3]

⇨ 47% of girls in 5th-12th grade reported wanting to lose weight because of magazine pictures.[12]

⇨ 69% of girls in 5th-12th grade reported that magazine pictures influenced their idea of a perfect body shape.[13]

⇨ 42% of 1st-3rd grade girls want to be thinner (Collins, 1991).

⇨ 81% of 10 year olds are afraid of being fat (Mellin et al., 1991).

Collins, M.E. (1991). Body figure perceptions and preferences among pre-adolescent children. International Journal of Eating Disorders, 199-208.

Mellin, L., McNutt, S., Hu, Y., Schreiber, G.B., Crawford, P., & Obarzanek, E. (1991). A longitudinal study of the dietary practices of black and white girls 9 and 10 years old at enrollment: The NHLBI growth and health study. Journal of Adolescent Health, 23-37.

For Women:

⇨ Women are much more likely than men to develop an eating disorder. Only an estimated five to 15 percent of people with anorexia or bulimia are male.[14]

⇨ An estimated 0.5 to 3.7 percent of women suffer from anorexia nervosa in their lifetime.[14] Research suggests that about 1% of female adolescents have anorexia.[15]

⇨ An estimated 1.1 to 4.2% of women have bulimia nervosa in their lifetime.[14]

⇨ An estimated two to 5% of Americans experience binge

1 *Mortality in Anorexia Nervosa*. American Journal of Psychiatry, 1995; 152 (7): 1073-4.

2 *Characteristics and Treatment of Patients with Chronic Eating Disorders*, by Dr. Greta Noordenbox, International Journal of Eating Disorders, Volume 10: 15-29, 2002.

3 The Renfrew Center Foundation for Eating Disorders, *Eating Disorders 101 Guide: A Summary of Issues, Statistics and Resources*, 2003.

4 *American Journal of Psychiatry*, Vol. 152 (7), July 1995, P. 1073-1074, Sullivan, Patrick F

5 Shisslak, C.M., Crago, M., & Estes, L.S. (1995). *The Spectrum of Eating Disturbances*. International Journal of Eating Disorders, 18 (3): 209-219.

6 *National Association of Anorexia Nervosa and Associated Disorders 10-year study*, 2000.

7 Public Health Service's Office in Women's Health, *Eating Disorders Information Sheet*, 2000.

8 Substance Abuse and Mental Health Services Administration (SAMHSA), The Center for Mental Health Services (CMHS), offices of the U.S. Department of Health and Human Services.

9 Carlat, D.J., Camargo. *Review of Bulimia Nervosa in Males*. American Journal of Psychiatry, 154, 1997.

10 American Psychological Association, 2001.

11 American Psychological Association, 2001.

12 *Prevention of Eating Problems with Elementary Children*, Michael Levine, USA Today, July 1998.

13 Ibid.

14 The National Institute of Mental Health: *Eating Disorders: Facts About Eating Disorders and the Search for Solutions*. Pub No. 01-4901. Accessed Feb. 2002. http://www.nimh.nih.gov/publicat/nedspdisorder.cfm.

15 *Anorexia Nervosa and Related Eating Disorders*, Inc. website. Accessed Feb. 2002. http://www.anred.com/

eating disorder in a 6-month period.[14]

⇨ About 50% of people who have had anorexia develop bulimia or bulimic patterns.[15]

⇨ 20% of people suffering from anorexia will prematurely die from complications related to their eating disorder, including suicide and heart problems.[18]

Mortality rates:

Although eating disorders have the highest mortality rate of any mental disorder, the mortality rates reported on those who suffer from eating disorders can vary considerably between studies and sources. Part of the reason why there is a large variance in the reported number of deaths caused by eating disorders is because those who suffer from an eating disorder may ultimately die of heart failure, organ failure, malnutrition or suicide. Often, the medical complications of death are reported instead of the eating disorder that compromised a person's health.

According to a study carried out by colleagues at the *American Journal of Psychiatry* (2009), crude mortality rates were:

⇨ 4% for anorexia nervosa

⇨ 3.9% for bulimia nervosa

⇨ 5.2% for eating disorder not otherwise specified

Crow, S.J., Peterson, C.B., Swanson, S.A., Raymond, N.C., Specker, S., Eckert, E.D., Mitchell, J.E. (2009) Increased mortality in bulimia nervosa and other eating disorders. American Journal of Psychiatry 166, 1342-1346.

Athletes:

⇨ Risk factors: in judged sports – sports that score participants – prevalence of eating disorders is 13% (compared with 3% in refereed sports).[19]

16. *Nutrition Journal*. March 31, 2006.
17. Neumark-Sztainer, D. (2005). *I'm, Like, SO Fat!*. New York: The Guilford Press. pp. 5.
18. The Renfrew Center Foundation for Eating Disorders, *Eating Disorders 101 Guide: A Summary of Issues, Statistics and Resources*, published September 2002, revised October 2003, http://www.renfrew.org
19. Zucker NL, Womble LG, Williamson DA, et al.

⇨ Significantly higher rates of eating disorders found in elite athletes (20%), than in a female control group (9%).[20]

⇨ Female athletes in aesthetic sports (e.g. gymnastics, ballet, figure skating) found to be at the highest risk for eating disorders.[20]

⇨ A comparison of the psychological profiles of athletes and those with anorexia found these factors in common: perfectionism, high self-expectations, competitiveness, hyperactivity, repetitive exercise

Protective factors for eating disorders in female college athletes. Eat Disorders 1999; 7: 207-218.
20. Sungot-Borgen, J. Torstveit, M.K. (2004) *Prevalence of ED in Elite Athletes is Higher than in the General Population*. Clinical Journal of Sport Medicine, 14(1), 25-32.
21. Bachner-Melman, R., Zohar, A, Ebstein, R, et.al. 2006. *How Anorexic-like are the Symptom and Personality Profiles of Aesthetic Athletes?* Medicine & Science in Sports & Exercise 38 No 4. 628-636.

routines, compulsiveness, drive, tendency toward depression, body image distortion, preoccupation with dieting and weight.[21]

⇨ The above information is reprinted with kind permission from ANAD (National Association of Anorexia Nervosa & Associated Disorders, Inc.). Please visit www.anad.org for further information.

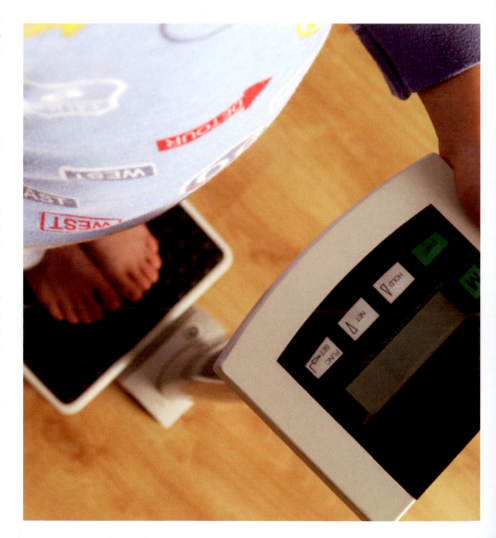

Triggers for boy anorexia

I have been asked many times 'Did you ever find out what caused Joe's anorexia?'. The straightforward answer is 'no'. However, we have a few ideas about what could have been contributing factors:

He went through a very early puberty. It is no coincidence that many cases of anorexia start in puberty, both in boys and girls. With girls the reason seems more obvious as they look in the mirror and see a more rounded shape developing. Boys tend to be more happy with their developing, more muscular, physique, but if a boy has a very early puberty he might not appreciate the changes that are happening to his body and making him different from his peers. In addition, the raging hormones can trigger irrational behaviour in either sex.

Joe was, and having recovered from his illness is still, a very talented sportsman. This is his explanation: 'I thought I would be an even better sportsman if I lost a little weight. I felt really good when I lost weight and to start with all my friends commented

on how good I looked. The trouble was it got out of control and I found I couldn't stop losing weight. I just got scared of eating in case I put weight back on.' There are numerous cases of sportsmen restricting their diet for their sport and developing an eating disorder. Consider jockeys, gymnasts, lightweight boxers, long-distance runners, cyclists and ballet dancers who can all justify restricting their diet to ensure they maintain an 'optimum' weight for their sport.

Joe is the eldest child of a complex family. He has one sibling, three half siblings and three stepsiblings. It is likely that he felt he was always the last in the pecking order of all these younger children. For years he may have been craving more of our attention without us realising. He always seemed such a happy boy with a healthy appetite, and who loved his sport. When I read *The Best Little Girl in the World* by Steven Levenkron it made me realise how an outwardly happy and well balanced child could actually be feeling very lonely and left out by the demands of other children within the family.

Research has shown that pre-term babies are more likely to suffer from behavioural difficulties including eating disorders. Joe was born six weeks prematurely so this could have been a contributory factor.

There could have been many other triggers of Joe's anorexia, but he didn't bring them to our attention. Of course we agonised about such things as our family structure, whether he was being overstretched at school, or being bullied, etc? It is important to note that anorexia can appear in any family setting and in any social situation. We are a large and complex family but many small nuclear families, who appear to have no problems, have been affected by a visit from anorexia. Children from

all walks of life are vulnerable. Some typical triggers might include:

⇨ An overweight child being teased or bullied at school. Comments might be made in jest and in a friendly manner, but then taken to heart.

⇨ A highly academic child might be bullied by less able children and see food as a way to control his life.

⇨ A less academic child might see weight loss as the only thing he can achieve positive results with.

⇨ A child whose parents are constantly dieting might follow suit.

⇨ A child who has seen an overweight parent or relative suffer a heart attack might seek to prevent this happening to him by cutting back on food.

⇨ Abuse within the family often leads to an eating disorder.

⇨ A death in the family can create a feeling of helplessness and loss of control. A child might find comfort in having control over food.

⇨ An over-protective or over dominant mother has often been blamed in the past for her child's eating disorder.

⇨ A passive or absent father has also been often cited as a reason for a child developing eating problems.

Social pressures might cause a child to start dieting and exercising. Within our culture young men who have a slim and athletic build are portrayed as being popular, attractive, healthy and successful in life. A young boy with puppy fat might feel he has to take drastic measures to achieve this image as soon as possible.

As well as the above-mentioned social triggers, eating disorders can also be triggered by chemical or biological factors. Chemical imbalances in the brain can lead to all sorts of behavioural disorders. It is also increasingly believed that there may be a genetic link, and certainly eating disorders seem to run in families.

The bottom line is that every case is different. No one type of person gets an eating disorder, and no two people with an eating disorder are exactly alike. The common features seem to be that people who develop eating disorders suffer from a very low self-esteem, and many find it difficult to express their true feelings or explain what is making them unhappy.

Of course we will never really know exactly what triggered Joe's illness, and like most parents of anorexic children we went through many months of agonising over what we could have done better to prevent our son almost starving himself to death. Joe's key worker made me feel much better when she made two points in our first meeting:

⇨ It is much more important to look forward, not back. What caused Joe's illness may well be totally irrelevant to his recovery and his future. Of course if we discovered, during the course of his therapy, that there was something in his life that was making him unhappy then we could endeavour to change it. In many cases of anorexia the initial triggers remain a complete mystery.

⇨ All families are dysfunctional in some way. However simple or complex your family set up, there are always disagreements and periods where some members are less happy than others are. Of course we should examine our family set up, and try to change if necessary, but we shouldn't assume that there must be something terribly wrong with our family simply because our son had developed anorexia. Family therapy is a very good forum for examining the family set up and discussing if any changes might be beneficial.

⇨ The above information is reprinted with kind permission from Boy Anorexia. Please visit www.boyanorexia.com for further information.

© Boy Anorexia 2013

'I'm a bulimic boy'

I'm in my mid-30s, male and bulimic. It's hard to know how common a combination this is. Reliable, up-to-date information is scarce. In 2005 the Eating Disorders Association estimated that ten to 20% of eating disorder sufferers in the UK were male. It may be a higher proportion if men are less willing than women to seek help.

Bulimia nervosa is characterised by a cycle of binge and purge: overeating, then getting rid of calories so as not to put on weight. That's in contrast to anorexia nervosa, which involves restricting eating in order to control weight and shape. But this can be a blurry distinction and in fact, I started by dieting and the bingeing came later.

I was 22 and had just left university. I'd never had much of a relationship with food at all. It was fuel. I ate when hungry. I liked some things and not others. But I paid it little attention.

Then one day I looked down while showering and thought I looked a bit fat. So the next day I took one sandwich to work instead of two. I made my breakfasts a little smaller. And my dinners. I started cycling a couple of extra miles each way on my commute (already a 17-mile round trip). I went running almost every lunchtime instead of twice a week.

That happened over perhaps two or three months. Not long, but long enough for the slide into disordered eating to be imperceptible on a day-to-day basis. I remember thinking at first that I was being healthy: keeping active and watching what I ate.

Then I started bingeing and any illusions that this was 'normal' were shattered. While my housemates went out on a Saturday night, I'd stay in, bake a cake and eat the lot before they got home. I had an overwhelming urge to eat and I had to satisfy it. I still get that urge almost every day. It's like a trance. Thoughts of consequences are banished (although I know very well what those consequences are) and if I give in I eat until I'm so full that I have to stop.

So what are the consequences? For me they've been much more damaging mentally than physically.

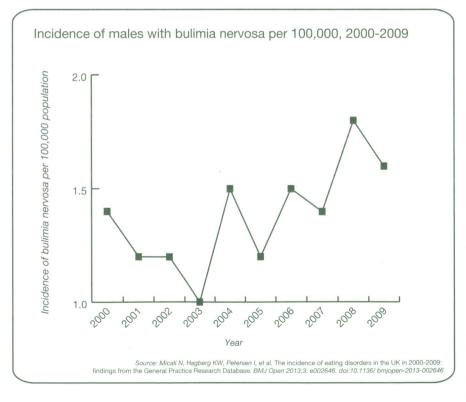

Incidence of males with bulimia nervosa per 100,000, 2000-2009

Source: Micali N, Hagberg KW, Petersen I, et al. The incidence of eating disorders in the UK in 2000-2009: findings from the General Practice Research Database. BMJ Open 2013;3: e002646. doi:10.1136/ bmjopen-2013-002646

Bulimia's often associated with bingeing followed by self-induced vomiting. Vomiting can cause severe tooth decay; you can go short of essential nutrients; and you can do all sorts of harm to the lining of your oesophagus.

But some bulimics – 6–8% according to David Barlow in his book *Abnormal psychology: an integrative approach* – over-exercise as a means of weight control. I'm one. The physical effects may be less pronounced but the psychological effects no less debilitating. It's a mental illness. I feel fit from cycling around 35 miles a day (and fitness is good cover for hiding my condition from almost everyone), but my head's a mess. I'm ashamed at my lack of self-control, and at the things I've done (eating food out of bins is nothing to be proud of no matter how much you hate waste).

I feel guilty because I'm withdrawn and I don't always show my wife the love that she deserves, even though she couldn't be more supportive and understanding. My self-esteem is rock-bottom and that affects all sorts of things, not least my work, where I lack confidence and take criticism too much to heart.

I've spent 12 years suffering on and off with depression because of my bulimia and that's very, very tiring. I devote so much emotional energy to trying to control my eating, or to dealing with its consequences, that I often have nothing left for anything or anyone else. That's no way to live. That's why finally, after more false dawns than I care to remember, I think I'm ready to get better.

Saying that scares me because it's easy to prophesise recovery but much harder to achieve it. Setting myself up for failure risks giving my self-esteem a further kicking. But I've been given a chance and I have to grab it.

That chance came unexpectedly, when I was knocked off my bike and broke a collar bone. No cycling for two months. I'd always dreaded this, but in fact it was a golden opportunity. If I carried on bingeing as usual (let's say two or three binges of 5,000 kcal each week) without cycling I was going to put on some serious weight. And that's the last thing a bulimic wants.

I'm back on the bike now, and while the collar bone has healed I can't claim to have recovered so fully from my eating disorder. But I'm heading the right way. After 12 years I was never going to be able to turn it off with the flick of some psychic switch, but the penny seems to have dropped and I realise now that it has to come from within. I have to want – and I mean really want, so much so that I'm willing to suffer – to get better. That means climbing the walls when the urge to binge strikes, while clinging to the knowledge that if I resist I'll feel immeasurably better the next day than if I give in.

Ultimately, for me at least, it comes down to finding self-control somewhere inside me. But I'm doing everything I can to get support. I've been to my GP and I'm hoping to get a course of cognitive behavioural therapy (the treatment recommended by the National Institute for Health and Clinical Excellence).

And I've started blogging about my experience. Getting my thoughts and feelings out helps me to make sense of them. And the idea that maybe someone in a similar position will read about my experience and find something helpful in it really gives me strength. If something positive can come out of all this, it would make me feel a little less as though the last 12 years have been wasted.

If you're suffering from an eating disorder or think you might be, tell someone. Get help. Don't wait until it becomes so embedded in your life that it's just 'normal'. It isn't. It's harmful. There are plenty of good web resources (start with Beat or Men Get Eating Disorders Too) and see your GP. Don't be ashamed. Facing it now will be much less shameful than the feeling of living with it for years.

4 April 2012

⇨ The above information is reproduced with kind permission of the Men's Health Forum from their website www.malehealth.co.uk.

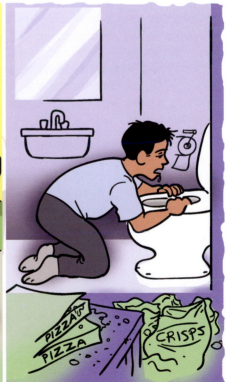

Can you tell if a friend has an eating disorder?

It's Eating Disorders Awareness week. Only a tenth of sufferers are anorexic, so look beyond body shape to spot the signs.

I found out during sixth form that three of my friends had had an eating disorder in their GCSE years. Each time, my immediate reaction – for which I now chide myself – was one of surprise: they'd always looked so healthy.

As someone who has since come through an eating disorder myself, and as a volunteer for Beat – the UK's leading eating disorder charity – I've spent years encouraging people to look beyond the visual to recognise the disease.

'Look out for physical and emotional symptoms: side-effects can include fatigue, difficulty concentrating, insomnia, frequent illness and mood swings'

Only 10% of eating disorders sufferers are anorexic – and easily identified by severe weight loss. Around 40% suffer from bulimia (binge eating and purging) and the remaining 50% from 'ednos' (eating disorder not otherwise specified, a category into which binge eating falls).

Though some people struggling with bulimia or ednos are underweight, the majority have a normal BMI, while some are overweight. When I heard my friends' admissions, I instantly fell into the trap of equating 'eating disorder' with 'emaciation', forming a host of regrettable assumptions about their experiences.

It's often assumed that anorexia is fuelled by vanity and a desire to emulate skinny celebrities. In reality, eating disorders, including anorexia, are serious mental health problems, triggered by a complex interplay of low self-worth, difficulties in coping with problems and – possibly – genetics.

To recognise and understand these conditions, we need to look for behavioural signs as well as weight changes. For example, a friend with an eating disorder may become more withdrawn, preferring to spend time alone rather than engage in social situations they used to enjoy.

They may become extremely anxious at meal times and try to get out of events that revolve around food – you may notice they have taken to eating alone.

An obsession with calories and fat content can be an indicator, as can strict avoidance of certain food groups.

Some people with eating disorders – particularly anorexia – choose to engage in lengthy discussions about food, sometimes as a way of indulging through conversation, and sometimes to find out more about others' eating habits against which they can measure their own.

Look out for physical and emotional symptoms: side-effects can include fatigue, difficulty concentrating, insomnia, frequent illness and mood swings.

If you suspect a friend has an eating disorder and you want to help, you'll need to raise the subject gently. Reading through these dos and don'ts before broaching the topic will help, but don't beat yourself up if the conversation doesn't go as well as you'd hoped: your friend will appreciate your concern.

Offering to go with your friend to a GP appointment can be a helpful first step, as GPs refer people on to services that can help them.

Peer-to-peer support can be a really valuable way of complementing professional services. Student Run Self Help (SRSH) is a network of groups run by trained students in many universities across the UK. It aims to provide a safe, confidential space for students with eating disorders to share their experiences; attendance does not require a diagnosis. Going to groups for the first time can be daunting, so offering to accompany your friend might give them the confidence to turn up.

'When students face mental health problems, they are most likely to turn to their friends for support,' says SRSH founding director Nicola Byrom. 'The problems faced by young people with eating disorders are often wrapped around issues of low self-esteem, so knowing that you have friends there to support you can make the world of difference.'

'When students face mental health problems, they are most likely to turn to their friends for support... knowing you have friends there to support you can make the world of difference'

Recovery can be a slow process – you'll need patience as well as understanding to help rescue your friend from the turmoil they are going through.

11 February 2013

⇨ The above article is reprinted with kind permission from *The Guardian*. Please visit www.guardian.co.uk for further information.

Five things you may not have known about eating disorders in children...

1. The most commonly cited trigger for eating disorders in children is bullying. A survey carried out by Beat of over 600 people revealed that 65% felt bullying had contributed to their eating disorder. One of our own eating disorder centres, Rhodes Farm, also conducted a survey on patients (eight- to 18-years-old) over the last four years to see if there were any emergent patterns on the reasons why children develop eating disorders. In the younger age group (eight- to 18-years-old), the most common factor cited was bullying. 42% of the children claimed that they were being bullied, with half of them being bullied about their weight.

2. Some research suggests a link between the development of a childhood eating disorder and healthy eating advice. It is also a factor that has been mentioned by some children treated at Rhodes Farm in the last few years. However, it is important to remember that healthy eating talks do not cause eating disorders in children. Most children will just listen to the talks and consider the advice (or not!). Unfortunately, some children, with underlying emotional worries or issues, may use their new knowledge and awareness in ways not intended, for example restricting calories or over-exercising.

3. The most common form of therapy for children and teenagers with eating disorders is family therapy. After bullying, one of the most common underlying factors that can trigger an eating disorder are issues in a child's family life. This could range from bereavement, a divorce or even moving home for the first time. Family therapy can provide space and time for a child and members of their family to talk and discuss openly any problems that have occurred. We reassure families we work with that family therapy is not a 'blame game' – it is safe space where the child and loved ones can work through problems together.

4. Many children will not tell anyone about their eating disorder. Eating disorders are a very secretive illness. Many suffer in silence and it is only when they became very ill that action is taken. Here are some statistics from Beat:

⇨ 1% of children felt they could talk to their parents about their eating-related concerns

⇨ 9% of children felt they might be able to talk to someone at school

⇨ 17% of children felt they might be able to talk to a doctor or nurse

⇨ 92% of children felt they couldn't tell anyone

These stats remind us why it is so important to know the signs and symptoms.

5. Some GPs may not always recognise a child's condition as an eating disorder. If you are concerned about your child and your GP does not see problems with your child's eating behaviour, it might be worth seeking advice or a second opinion from an eating disorder specialist. A GP may not have experience of identifying childhood eating disorders so they may not always spot it straight away. Remember, the earlier the diagnosis, the better chance of recovery.

23 April 2012

⇨ The above information is reprinted with kind permission from Care UK. Please visit www. careukeatingdisorders.com for further information.

Children aged five treated for 'eating disorders'

Children as young as five are being treated for eating disorders, according to new figures, but one charity tells Channel 4 News it would be 'very surprised' if children that young had anorexia.

More than 2,000 children have received treatment for eating disorders in the past three years.

Statistics show that nearly 600 children under the age of 13 were treated in hospital in England, including 197 aged between five and nine, after developing eating disorders.

About three in every 100,000 children under 13 in the UK and Ireland have some sort of eating disorder, according to a study conducted by experts from University College London's Institute for Child Health.

Some NHS hospitals treating such patients refused to provide any data while others would only release figures for children admitted after becoming dangerously thin, excluding those undergoing psychiatric therapy as outpatients.

The findings come after experts called earlier this year for urgent action to improve the detection of eating disorders in children.

Charity Beat provides support for adults and young people with eating disorders.

Head of services Francis Burrows told Channel 4 News he would be 'very surprised' if children aged five were suffering from such a 'serious mental illness' as anorexia.

He pointed out that the figures included all children being treated in a hospital setting for various problems with eating. But Mr Burrows said more could be done to support young people who had concerns about their body image.

'Parents need to think if they're constantly dieting what kind of role model that is setting for their children.

'But it isn't just about food and eating. Anorexia is a severe mental illness and bullying is often cited as a cause so it's important to create a loving and supportive environment and check children are doing well at school,' he said.

He said there was evidence to show that the sooner eating disorders were treated the more likely the individual was to recover and urged anyone worried about a loved one to seek help.

A Department of Health spokeswoman said: 'We are committed to improving mental health among the whole population.

'That is why we are providing around £400 million over the next four years to expand psychological therapies, including a specific programme for children and young people. Early intervention is essential for those with eating disorders.'

1 August 2011

⇨ The above information is reprinted with kind permission from Channel 4. Please visit www.channel4.com for further information.

Eating disorder admissions

2,290 eating disorder admissions in England, 2011-2012

Who

Children and teenagers aged 10 to 19 accounted for 55% of the total eating disorder admissions. This is up from 49% in 2010-2011

Women accounted for 91% of all eating disorder admissions. This is compared to 88% in the previous 12 months.

What

Anorexia accounted for 74% of all eating disorder admissions. Bulimia accounted for 7%. The remaining 19% were for 'other eating disorders' such as overeating or vomitting associated with other psychological disturbances.

Where

The North East had the highest number of admissions by population size at 5.8 per 100,000 (150 admissions).

London had the highest number of total admissions at 440 per 100,000 (5.6 per 100,000).

Source: Eating disorder hospital admissions rise by 16 per cent in a year. Health & Social Care Information Centre, October 11 2012.

Faddy eating: should you worry?

For some children, faddy eating means refusing all types of fruit and vegetables. Others want the same food at every meal, or insist on food of a certain colour.

'Most pre-school children will, at some time, experience some problems over eating,' explains Claudine Fox, co-author of a Royal College of Psychiatrists publication aimed at helping parents, called *Eating Problems in Children* (Gaskell).

'Some may only eat a small number of different foods or eat very little or sometimes refuse to eat altogether. But it will probably be a passing phase.'

Professor Marie Reid, clinical psychologist at Queen Margaret University College, Edinburgh, says selective eaters are often quite sensitive. A bad experience when eating – for example, choking when weaning – can also be a cause. Sibling rivalry and attention seeking can also be triggers.

Families living with a faddy eater often find themselves under additional stress when there's a change in routine. Holidays abroad can be difficult and faddy children may avoid sleepovers or friends' birthday parties because of food concerns. Food is one of the few things that a child has control over and refusing to eat or rejecting foods are common 'assertive' behaviours. Experts agree this rarely leads to eating disorders.

'If the child is thriving and there are no problems with growth and development, it is better to leave well alone. More than likely they will grow out of it,' adds Claudine. Anita Bean, registered nutritionist and author of *Healthy Eating for Kids* (A & C Black) agrees. 'Children do not voluntarily starve themselves,' she says. 'They are programmed for survival – as long as there is food available, children will make sure they get enough.'

'Some children are very good at using food to wind up their parents. They know that food refusal results in attention, even unfavourable, and so a vicious cycle sets up.' Vivien Wigg, Senior Paediatric Dietician at Great Ormond Street Hospital, sees many children who are afraid or suspicious of new foods (called neophobia). She says it may take months or even years before they are ready to try new things.

Parents of faddy eaters worry that if it carries on long-term, it could stunt development. However, children with selective eating have a very good long-term outlook, adds Claudine. Their diets usually contain enough protein, carbohydrates, fat, vitamins and minerals so they will be healthy and grow normally, she says. 'If your child is not upset or worried about eating, then there is little that you need to do. You should try to accept the narrow diet, expecting that it will become wider in time.'

By the time they become teenagers, almost all will have grown out of faddy eating. Even the approximate 1% who carry on to be selective eaters as adults don't appear to have any long-term consequences.

Faddy eating tips:

Dos...

⇨ Do have structured meal times. Don't rush. Avoid talking about food.

⇨ Do let your children see that you enjoy eating healthy meals. 'They are more likely to eat foods that they have seen you eat,' explains Anita.

⇨ Do praise your child when they try something new – but don't overdo it.

⇨ Do get your children involved in cooking, advises Anita. 'This will increase their interest in the food, and they're more likely to eat a meal they've helped prepare.'

⇨ Do think of different ways to present foods, says Vivien: 'Your child may refuse fresh tomato but accept a tomato-based pizza, for example. Some parents disguise fruit and vegetables, pureeing vegetables into a mince-based dish, or using fruit purees in jellies and in cooking.'

⇨ Do set a time limit of, say 20-30 minutes for the meal. If the food isn't eaten, take it away.

Don'ts...

⇨ 'Don't ever bribe children,' warns Vivien. 'It's a very common mistake to make but avoid it at all costs, particularly rewarding children with a pudding.'

⇨ Don't get cross: refusing food loses its appeal if you don't react, explains Anita.

⇨ Don't provide an alternative meal. 'Just remove the meal and make no comment,' says Vivien. 'Offer bread and butter

Brussel sprouts are good for you!

and perhaps a glass of milk but never cook multiple meals as your child could misconstrue it as a game.'

⇨ Don't let your child fill up between meals on snacks, juice and fizzy drinks.

⇨ Don't let your child hear you talking about how fussy they are,' warns Vivien. 'This will only make an issue of their eating habits and make them feel isolated and singled out.'

Try these…

⇨ Make sure your child is hungry before meal times.

⇨ Let them serve themselves. Put the food in dishes so they can choose how much to take.

⇨ Think small: a big pile of food on the plate can be off-putting for children. Try tiny broccoli florets, small squares of toast, super-thin apple slices.

⇨ Serve a new food with a food they like: mix an unfamiliar food, like peppers, into pasta sauce, soup or curry – but don't try and hide them under other foods otherwise you risk the whole meal being rejected.

⇨ Keep trying! If a food is rejected, it doesn't mean they will never eat it. Children's tastes do change over time. It can take up to eight to ten attempts to get a child to eat a new food.

⇨ Invite other children round who you know eat heartily! Experiments have shown that children often copy their peers at meal times.

⇨ The above information is reprinted with kind permission from Family Lives. Please visit www.familylives.org.uk for further information.

What really killed Amy Winehouse was the eating disorder bulimia, her brother Alex claims

The singer's elder brother says years of suffering from an eating disorder left Amy 'weaker and more susceptible'.

The underlying cause of Amy Winehouse's premature death at the age of 27 was the eating disorder bulimia, her brother has claimed.

The singer's older brother Alex Winehouse, 33, said in an interview that years of suffering from bulimia left Amy 'weaker and more susceptible' to the physical impact of her alcohol and drug addictions.

A coroner's verdict recorded that the 'Rehab' singer died of 'alcohol toxicity' after drinking too much.

'She would have died eventually, the way she was going,' Alex told the *Observer*. 'But what really killed her was the bulimia… Had she not had an eating disorder, she would have been physically stronger.'

'She suffered from bulimia very badly. That's not, like, a revelation – you knew just by looking at her'

Bulimia is an eating disorder characterised by episodes of bingeing followed by self-induced vomiting. Alex claims Amy was a sufferer from her late teens until her death at the age of 27.

'She suffered from bulimia very badly. That's not, like, a revelation – you knew just by looking at her,' he said.

She was influenced, he said, by her peers, who were 'all doing it', at the age of 17. 'They'd put loads of rich sauces on their food, scarf it down and throw it up. They stopped doing it, but Amy never really did,' he said.

'Had she not had an eating disorder, she would have been physically stronger'

Amy, who won five Grammy awards for her breakthrough album Back to Black, was found dead at her flat in Camden, north London, on 23 July 2011.

An inquest recorded a verdict of misadventure after finding that she had 416 mg of alcohol per decilitre in her blood – more than five times the legal drink-drive limit.

Since her death, her father Mitch and her brother Alex have set up the Amy Winehouse Foundation, which works to prevent the effects of drug and alcohol misuse on young people.

An exhibition of family photographs and objects belonging to the singer has been put together by Mitch and Alex Winehouse at the Jewish Museum in London, opening next month.

24 June 2013

⇨ The above information is reprinted with kind permission from *The Independent*. Please visit www.independent.co.uk for further information.

Chapter 2 · Media influence

The media & eating disorders

By Deanne Jade, National Centre For Eating Disorders. Acknowledgement: The British Medical Association, Eating Disorders Body Image and The Media

The media are held responsible for the supposed growth of eating disorders in the country. To what extent is this true? In this short article I would like to separate myth from fact, and to provide the reader with some articles that might help them decide which is cause and which is effect.

What is the media?

The media is an important aspect of life in our culture. About 95% of people own a TV set and watch for an average of three to four hours per day. By the end of the last century over 60% of men and 50% of women read a newspaper each day and nearly half of all girls, from the age of seven read a girls' magazine each week. In addition, people interact with a wide variety of other media such as music delivered by CDs or videos, and communications via personal computers.

Each form of medium has a different purpose and content. The media

seek to inform us, persuade us, entertain us and change us. The media also seeks to engage large groups of people so that advertisers can sell them products or services by making them desirable. Other institutions such as governments also engage the public via the media to make ideas and values desirable. Institutions from politics to corporations can use the media to influence our behaviour. We can trace our involvement with the media back to the drum messages of the Indians, the shouts of the town crier. All that has changed are the multitudinous ways in which information passes to us and the increasing sophistication of the media providers.

The argument about whether the media shape society or merely reflect current or nascent trends is constantly under debate. Before the Second World War, it was believed that the media 'injects' values and morals into society. However, social research in the 1960s showed that the audience is not a passive receiver of moral values. Society is constructed of many different subcultures, classified by factors such as race, social class, political outlook, adhesion to value systems such as 'vegetarianism' or lifestyles (such as 'cocooners'). These differing social groups select and filter information and reject messages that are not consistent with the values of that group. On the other hand, irrespective of social

clusters, research has shown that it is those with low confidence and self-esteem within each group who are most influenced by media communications.

So there have been many debates about the influence of the media and social behaviour, for example sexual morality or violence. We recognise, as a result of these debates, that the interaction between message and response is complex and audience dependent. To quote the BMA report on eating disorders, body image and the media:

'In a media-saturated culture, the argument that long-term exposure can help shape the world views of particular sections of the audience is one that merits consideration; however, the EXTENT to which the media contribute to the personal identity remains unclear and is subject to continuing academic debate...the media do not, by their very definition, provide pure experience of the world but channel our experience of it in particular ways.'

In other words, all research into the media must take into account the different levels of attention, and interpretation of individuals with different motivations, personalities, immediate situations and socio-cultural contexts who bring different information processing strategies to the task.

The latest 'POSTMODERN' thinking on the role of media is that it provides learning that is incidental rather than direct, and it is a significant part of the acculturation process.

Now the battle centres on a new morality of food and eating. We accuse the media, by glorifying the culture of thinness, of causing an epidemic of eating distress, especially among young women. The media denies culpability, or at least responsibility for doing anything about it. Kelly Brownell, a US expert in eating disorders, argues that the media contribute to a toxic environment in which eating disorders may be more likely to occur. This is because of the 'Damaging Paradox' of modern society in which the media promotes, in a compelling manner, a low-weight, sculptured ideal body.

At the same time the environment provides an increasing array of foods high in fat and calories, with compelling pressures to consume these products. As a result we are getting heavier, and the gap between the ideal and normal body weight is giving rise to anxiety. We seek to reduce this anxiety by reducing our body weight, the preferred method being to go on a diet, since we believe that weight IS under our control and, in addition we believe that once weight is lost it should not be regained. But dieting causes rebound binge eating and attempts to deal with this, by going on further diets, will lead many people into a disturbed relationship with food.

There are other dangers arising from this cultural paradox. The models and actors who promote consumption of these calorie-laden foods are usually slim and attractive, which would not be possible in a real world if they actually ate these foods. This will add to the cultural confusion, which is said to nurture the onset of eating distress. To what extent are these accusations true?

⇨ The above information is reprinted with kind permission from The National Centre for Eating Disorders. Please visit www.eating-disorders.org.uk for further information.

Talent scouts troll eating disorder clinic to recruit skinny models

By Samantha Chang

Unscrupulous modelling scouts are under fire after being caught trolling Sweden's largest eating-disorder clinic in Stockholm for modelling prospects.

'People have stood outside our clinic and tried to pick up our girls because they know they are very thin,' Dr. Anna-Maria told *The Local* 18 April. 'We think this is repugnant. It sends the wrong signals when the girls are being treated for eating disorders.'

In one instance, a modelling scout approached a 14-year-old girl suffering from anorexia. In another incident, a scout tried to recruit an emaciated young woman who was in a wheelchair due to starvation-induced poor health.

'If these allegations are true, it's despicable,' says psychologist Andreas Birgegård, chair of the Swedish Anorexia and Bulimia Society. 'For people who have an illness centred around weight and looks, it's catastrophic to throw them into a business that focuses on exactly those things.'

It's unclear how many modelling agencies were involved in the bizarre scandal. However, it has long been known that anorexia, bulimia and other eating disorders are rampant in the fashion industry, where being a size zero is the holy grail.

Runway models have admitted to extreme dieting, starvation, excessive smoking, drug use and laxative abuse in an attempt to achieve the rail-thin physique required in their jobs.

'Packs of cigarettes, daily colonics, laxatives, diet pills, Adderall, prescription drugs that suppress the appetite [are some of the weight-loss techniques],' Russian model Kira Dikhtyar told Fox News.

'I've heard stories that some modelling agents encourage girls to do speed and cocaine in order to speed up metabolism and eat less.'

While the fashion industry has been making an attempt to promote a healthier body image by banning the use of anorexic-looking models, insiders say the aesthetic ideal of the waif-like, size-zero model will always be in vogue.

19 April 2013

⇨ The above information is reprinted with kind permission from Examiner.com.

Company magazine's faux pas

By Harriet Williamson

The fashion industry is constantly under fire for its perceived permissiveness with regard to the promotion of unhealthily thin female bodies, both on the catwalks and in the pages of fashion publications. In April 2013, the head doctor at Sweden's largest eating disorder treatment centre spoke out about modelling scouts accosting her patients, an example of the dark underside of fashion's reputation for worshipping the super-skinny. Research from the National Institute of Health and Clinical Excellence states that 1.6 million people in the UK currently suffer from an eating disorder, which provides a good indication of why fashion publications (among other media sources) should do all they can to place emphasis on varied bodies, not just the thin ones.

As a devoted *Company* reader, it was with a mixture of disappointment and disgust that I read *This Is Skinny Club*, an anonymous opinion piece in their June issue. 'Anon' describes how she lies to close friends about what she has eaten to avoid their concern, forces herself to exercise even when watching TV, and spends 90% of her life denying herself food. These behaviours are worryingly familiar to those who have experience of eating disorders, whether as sufferers or as friends and family of someone suffering. Of course, the views of the anonymous contributor do not automatically reflect that of *Company* itself, but the irony of their decision to print this article in the so-called *Feminism Issue 2013* was not lost on readers. Lancaster student and beauty blogger Ebony L. Nash remarks that 'to be so blasé about something so potentially devastating is just terrible journalism'. Her blog post can be found here: http://eInfashion.com/this-is-skinny-club-company-magazine/. Eating disordered behaviour is not a 'club' and should not be championed in a widely-read magazine with impunity. Anon's justification for her regimented lifestyle, that she can 'parade around in a denim mini-dress with Alexa-worthy pins' serves to normalise and make desirable the kind of behaviour that those who have suffered with anorexia must spend painful years unlearning.

I expected the article to be accompanied by a message about maintaining positive body image, an encouragement to eat in a balanced and healthy manner, or at least some information on what constitutes an eating disorder and how to get help. *Company* provided no trigger warning or disclaimer, only a space for comment at http://www.company.co.uk/magazine-hq/theskinnymyth, encouraging readers to state whether they found the piece 'offensive' or 'refreshingly honest'. Their response, published on their Facebook page *The Company Collective* after strong reactions from many readers, does little to redeem the situation. The assertion that 'the girl in the story is not anorexic she is simply always watching what she eats' is small

comfort when her article, filled with positive messages about eating disorder behaviour, has already reached a substantial readership.

I firmly believe that one can appreciate fashion and still take a stand against the shameless promotion of unrealistic and damaging body expectations. After struggling with a mixture of anorexia and bulimia for seven years, I am finally able to celebrate my love of clothing and style without extending that affection to the size of those who march the catwalks. In the world of fashion things are changing, H&M's use of size 12 model Jennie Runk in their 2013 beachwear campaign and refusal to label the collection as 'plus size' providing a good example of this. I remain disappointed with *Company*'s decision to print such an immensely triggering article, but hopeful that they will balance this out with a future feature on body confidence or the kind of support available for eating disorders. 'Anon' may believe that 'nothing tastes as good as skinny feels' but she's obviously never had my mum's coffee and walnut cake.

31 May 2013

⇨ The above article is reprinted with kind permission from *The Huffington Post (UK)*. Please visit www.huffingtonpost.co.uk for further information.

Diet of gossip magazines linked to teenage eating disorders

By Carolyn Allen

Teenagers who read gossip magazines are more likely to engage in unhealthy eating behaviours such as binge eating, skipping meals or making themselves sick after meals, according to an ESRC-funded study.

These unhealthy eating behaviours can lead to serious eating disorders, such as anorexia or bulimia, which are a growing public health problem in the UK. Beat, the charity behind Eating Disorders Awareness Week, says that the most accurate statistics available suggest that 1.6 million people in the UK suffer from an eating disorder, but that the figure could be much higher.

The study, the first to identify an association between media exposure and changes in eating behaviour in teenagers, was led by Dr James White, a research associate at DECIPHer (Centre for the Development and Evaluation of Complex Interventions for Public Health Improvement).

The researchers asked over 500 youngsters from South Wales aged between 11 and 16 to record their eating patterns – including whether they were skipping meals, making themselves sick after eating, or binge eating. Six months later, the teenagers were asked for the same information so that the researchers could identify any changes in eating patterns.

The youngsters were also asked what types of television programmes they regularly watched and how often they looked at magazines about women's fashion, health and fitness, men's issues and gossip.

The results showed that adolescents – both boys and girls – who had looked at gossip magazines most often during the study, were also most likely to report worrying changes in eating behaviours. In contrast, exposure to television or to other types of magazines appeared to have no effect.

Even after taking into account other risk factors for eating disorders, such as body mass index and the amount of pressure that the teenagers felt they were under from the media to lose weight, gossip magazines remained a significant influence.

Previous research has shown that exposure to unrealistic ideals such as super-thin models increases the risk of people feeling dissatisfied with what they look like – one of the strongest factors associated with eating disorders. This has led to calls from organisations such as the Royal College of Psychiatrists for fashion magazines to feature more average-sized models and for warning symbols on digitally altered photographs.

But this study goes a step further by looking directly at changes in eating behaviour, and it shows that the type of images found in gossip magazines may have a greater impact on teenage boys and girls.

And, as the researchers found no link between the media pressure that teenagers perceived and the changes in eating behaviour, the teenagers appear to be unaware that they are being influenced in this way.

'What distinguishes gossip magazines is the way they ridicule celebrities who are overweight or even just don't conform to unrealistic ideals,' said Dr White. 'And at the same time they praise celebrities for losing weight. That combination of messages of 'fat is bad', 'thin is good' seems to be a particularly potent influence on vulnerable teenagers.'

'This study suggests that there should be greater awareness of the potential impact that exposure to the kind of images of celebrities and models in gossip magazines can have on adolescents' eating habits.'

20 February 2012

⇨ The above information is reprinted with kind permission from the Economic and Social Research Council. Please visit http://www.esrc.ac.uk/impacts-and-findings/features-casestudies/features/19167/Diet_of_gossip_magazines_linked_to_teenage_eating_disorders.aspx for further information.

© ESRC 2013

'Thinspo' anxiety: veiled anorexia in social media form

By Ryan Rivera

There's a growing movement online that is unfortunately causing fairly drastic consequences. It's called the 'Thinspo' movement, short for 'Thinspiration', (a portmanteau of 'thin' and 'inspiration') and it's taking over social media websites.

'Thinspo' is the act of viewing photos of women that are incredibly skinny – often with bones protruding out of their skin – and claiming that the photos are inspiration to get thin and exercise. The problem is that 'Thinspo' isn't health related at all. Rather, it's veiled anorexia that is unfortunately gaining popularity due to a lack of understanding of the social implications.

'Thinspo' and pro-ana

In many ways, 'Thinspo' is simply the next evolution of the pro-anorexia groups that caused significant problems during the last few decades. 'Thinspo' photos are women in the lowest 5% of body weight, often in the lowest 1%, and are spread through Pinterest, Twitter, and other social media sites.

What is making 'Thinspo' such a problem is that not everyone that uses the term or spreads the photos is sharing women that are 'unhealthy' thin. Many are simply fit, or in general good shape. There is another online sensation, known as 'fitspo' that – while still promoting the idea that all women need to be young and fit – shows photos of much healthier women that happen to be at the height of fitness.

Some of the 'Thinspo' tags are also photos of 'fitspo', and that means that not everyone using the phrase or promoting the idea even knows that they are spreading pro-ana. Many simply think they're promoting fitness, and so they share these photos and use the phrase openly, without regard to the consequences.

Unfortunately, 'true Thinspo' is much worse, and unfortunately many of those posting healthy 'Thinspo' are at risk for developing further body dysmorphic disorder and potentially posting photos of thinner and thinner women. The true promoters of 'Thinspo' often post photos of women with severe anorexia or weight problems, highlighting features that are nearly impossible for a healthy woman, including:

⇨ Thighs that are several inches from touching.

⇨ Bone ribs with no muscle mass.

⇨ Pronounced neck bones.

Many of the photos are photoshopped to appear even thinner. 'Thinspo' supporters also post several 'inspirational' quotes along with photos of the bones of deceased women. One only needs to look at the photos connected to the hash-tag to see the problem.

A study conducted by the Center for Eating Disorders at Sheppard Pratt in Maryland (2012) surveyed 600 Facebook users, aged between 16 and 40 and found that:

- Over 50% of those surveyed said that Facebook makes them more self-conscious about their bodies and their weight.

- 40% of men said they had posted negative comments about their own bodies, compared to 20% of women.

- 8% of people surveyed admit to logging on to Facebook at least once a day.

What 'Thinspo' does

Without awareness about what 'Thinspo' truly is and how it is promoting severe eating disorders among young women, there is going to be a serious problem. This is already a community that's growing rapidly, partly because of a lack of knowledge about what the 'Thinspo' movement is really designed to do, and unfortunately many women are finding that they are being roped into the 'Thinspo' movement accidentally, believing that they're taking part in a campaign to simply lose weight. The photos may start out with women that are simply thin but otherwise fit and healthy, but over time they risk growing thinner, as well as promoting an idea with other women that may be more prone to eating disorders.

Overall, 'Thinspo' is a serious problem that is quickly getting out of hand, and something that parents and educators need to address before the issue becomes out of control.

About the author: Ryan Rivera has seen the effects of anxiety on eating disorders and vice versa. He runs a website about reducing anxiety at www.calmclinic.com.

9 April 2013

⇨ The above information is reprinted with kind permission from The National Centre for Eating Disorders. Please visit www.eating-disorders.org.uk for further information.

What are pro-ana and pro-mia sites and what can we do about them?

There is a whole language around eating disorders that sounds like Greek to a lot of us:

⇨ Pro-ana – website that promotes anorexia

⇨ Pro-mia – website that promotes bulimia

⇨ Thinspiration/Thinspo – images to inspire weight loss

⇨ Fitspiration/Fitspo – images to inspire exercise/body building.

What are pro-ana and pro-mia sites?

Pro-ana and pro-mia sites are websites that promote anorexic and bulimic lifestyles. Set up by people with eating disorders looking to validate their illness and seeking support to continue with their eating disorder from fellow sufferers, these sites vary hugely in their precise content. They are often a forum for people to exchange pictures and weight loss or purging tips and to encourage one another's weight loss.

Who uses pro-ana and pro-mia sites?

These sites are often a refuge for people suffering from eating disorders. It's common for sufferers to feel quite isolated having pushed away their family and friends preferring to seek out like-minded individuals online. There are over 500 such sites and the latest studies predict that they attract more than 500,000 unique visitors a year of which the majority are teenage girls and one in five are aged between six and 11.

Why are they dangerous?

These sites are dangerous because they encourage the users to embrace eating disorders – seeing them as a lifestyle choice rather than the serious mental health condition which they actually are. The sites share tips and tricks designed to exacerbate eating disorders and there is often a support network which will encourage people to consume ever fewer calories, or purge longer and harder. With most things in life, if you have a good teacher and a good support network then your skills in and dedication to a particular topic will increase more quickly and this is true also of anorexia nervosa and bulimia nervosa, whose onset can be expedited and exacerbated by pro-ana and pro-mia sites. The sites also make recovery far harder as they contradict anything a young person may be told about the benefits of recovery and the downsides of eating disorders.

Highlight alternative sources of information

Many young people come across these sites as they have body image issues or the early symptoms of an eating disorder and are looking for more information or support, coming across a pro-ana site can catapult them into a terrifying new world where their eating disorder may rapidly develop even if they don't intend for that to happen. As such, it's important that we make it clear to young people where there are trusted sources of information and support about eating disorders – such as the Beat website and helpline (0845 634 7650). Also let them know that you're always happy to talk to them about concerns of this type.

Teach young people that eating disorders are serious mental health conditions

Ensure that young people understand that eating disorders are serious mental health conditions and not lifestyle choices as suggested by many pro-ana and pro-mia sites. Young people need to know that eating disorders can be fatal – anorexia nervosa being the most lethal of all mental health conditions with 10% of sufferers dying from complications of the illness or suicide.

Encourage young people to share their concerns about their friends

Often, friends can be the first to pick up the early warning signs of eating disorders – or may know that a friend is actively using pro-ana or pro-mia sites (though they are likely to refer to them in quite a different way). Explain to students who they should talk to if they're concerned, why it's important and what's likely to happen next. Teach students that a good friend is one who supports and looks out for a friend when they're in need and that by alerting a teacher or parent to the early signs of an eating disorder they could be saving their friend's life – even if their friend might be angry in the short term.

Act on your concerns

If you suspect that a young person is using these sites then it's vital that you intervene. Talk openly to the young person and allow them to share any concerns they currently have with you. You need to listen and ask plenty of open questions and be prepared to act on what you find out – this might mean referring the student to the lead teacher at school or the school counsellor. If you're a parent it might mean talking to the school or visiting your GP. But take some action and make sure the young person feels supported and cared for – and try to discourage them from using pro-ana sites, but be aware that cutting them off cold turkey or removing all of their internet access is likely to be counter-productive. Instead take a controlled, respectful approach, discussing with the young person concerned why such sites are a bad idea and agreeing restrictions on their use until they can be weaned off or find a more acceptable alternative.

⇨ This information is based on work supported by the National Institute of Health Research under its Programme Grants for Applied Research Scheme. Visit www.eatingdisordersadvice.co.uk for further support and ideas.

Should pro-eating disorder websites be banned?

Back in 2011 two of our journalists, Precious Adesina and Shanara Phillips decided they wanted to investigate pro-eating disorder websites and their influence on young people. As part of the story they spoke to Charlotte Allinson, the Young Person's Participation Manager at Beat, a charity that works with young people affected by eating disorders.

After speaking to Charlotte, Shanara and Precious decided to switch the focus of their article to how the media represent eating disorders, and the piece was published in issue two of *Pause* magazine. Following Tumblr's plan to ban pro-eating disorder and self-harm blogs, we thought we'd go back and publish what Charlotte had to say on the censorship of such websites when we spoke to her last year.:

On the Beat website, you make a statement about pro-eating disorder websites, saying that they are 'easy to come across' and that they can 'encourage people to avoid getting treatment and obtain ideas about how to maintain their disorder'. However, Beat also states they don't want them to be banned by law even though they are dangerous. Why is that?

'The difficulty is that for every one that gets shut down, another one will open. And what we have found by talking to people is that pro-eating disorder websites do offer people support in some way, if they haven't found somewhere like our site where they can get support as well. So by shutting them all down that would stop people from getting some kind of support. So it's a difficult one because the information isn't always correct on them.

What we have to try and do is make sure that our information is in all of the places where the wrong information might appear so that people can go on to our sites and profiles, and find responsible information and get the support that they need.'

So do you actually go onto the eating disorder websites and post your information then?

'We have profiles on all the social networking sites and if things are brought to our attention, such as a forum where there might be the wrong information, then we do post links to our websites, message boards and help lines.'

Do you believe that the pro-eating disorder websites and blogs have an effect on people's eating disorders?

'A number of the young people that we're in contact with did use pro-eating disorder websites when they were ill. Some people have said that it provided them with support, some people have told us it encouraged them to stay as they were, and other people have told us it encouraged them to get worse than they already were.'

So if you don't think they should be banned what actions do you think should be taken and by who?

'I think it's the responsibility of the Internet providers like Google and AOL to shut down the sites and make them difficult for people to get hold of. I don't think it's helpful for anybody to look at them to be honest.'

Obviously over the past few years things like blogging and social networking have really taken off, particularly with young people. Has this also led to an increase in pro-eating disorder websites, and has it made the situation worse for young people with eating disorders?

'The difficulty is that pro-eating disorder sites have been around for many, many years, but many newspapers and journalists will report on them as if they're new or even amusing, and almost draw attention to them again. So it's difficult to know whether people are using them or whether they're just being brought to people's attention again.

I mean there's lots of websites that tell people how to harm themselves in lots of different ways, and generally it'd be better if they weren't brought to people's attention, but I also understand the other side where people want them to be reported on because it is serious and they think they should be shut down, so it is a tricky situation.'

So how can these issues be raised in a responsible way?

'Well we do work with the media about not publishing damaging images. They don't always listen to us but that is something that we do. We try and work with journalists, TV, newspapers and magazines and we're also very careful about what information our media contacts and young ambassadors give out to people.

They don't give out details of how low a weight they got to if they had anorexia. They don't provide pictures of themselves at a low weight, they don't give people specific details of how they self-harmed because we don't want to trigger that in anybody else or make somebody think of a new way to harm themselves.'

⇨ The above information is reprinted with kind permission from Headliners. Please visit www.headliners.org for further information.

© *Headliners 2013*

A disorder of the mind and body

Consistently taxing, occasionally distressing, but always inspiring. Jethro Thompson has first-hand experience treating a much-misunderstood type of affliction: eating disorders.

By Jethro Thompson

When I tell people that my summer job is working on a ward for eating disorders, I invariably get one of two responses. 'But you're an English student!' is probably fair enough. More commonly, however, I am faced with 'that sounds grim'.

It's not grim. It can be taxing, at times distressing, but 'grim' implies a uniform grey, stifling atmosphere of depression which I've not encountered. People do get better and make full recoveries. To bite the clichéd bullet, working on the unit is interesting and rewarding too. Coming to university means that I am away from the ward for months at a time and returning in the next vacation and meeting patients who are noticeably recovering can be truly inspiring.

Eating disorders, particularly anorexia nervosa, are terrible illnesses that attack a person on all fronts. When the body is starved, the brain shrinks and basic comprehension is impaired, major organs are wasted away and bone density drops irreversibly. The solution can seem so simple: 'just bloody eat'.

Every case is complex and different, however. For someone with an eating disorder, there are four main behaviours that can contribute to weight loss: restricting food intake, vomiting, laxative abuse and excessive exercise. A sufferer may feel overwhelming compulsion to engage in one or more of these activities.

Eating disorders can also be accompanied by other mental health problems – depression is common and personality disorders can make treatment difficult. Many patients I've spoken to have described an internal 'voice' (though not literal auditory hallucinations) that produces and feeds on a patient's doubts and fears concerning eating. It often manifests itself in physical delusions – a sufferer might pinch skin on an emaciated arm and view it as evidence of obesity. In fact, almost every patient considers themselves to be the biggest on the unit, even though many can easily recognise the effects of malnutrition and need for weight gain in others.

The causes of anorexia nervosa are as varied as its symptoms. Someone in a difficult or stressful situation, perhaps caught in the crossfire of family rows at home or drowning under pressure at university, might turn to eating disorder behaviours as a means of establishing control over some part of their life. The influences of the media and the fashion industry have an impact, particularly for those attempting a career in modelling. Certainly, our culture has a damaging obsession with thinness and weight loss, but as a cause of eating disorders this factor is often overstated.

Where I work, each patient (and member of staff) makes their own laminated placemat covered in pictures of family, friends, pets and motivational messages to have something comforting and personal as a distraction during meal times. When a patient is discharged, their placemat goes up on the wall as a very real reminder of the patients that have recovered and left the unit. There is a temptation to be demoralised when you spot the past mats of a current, returned patient pinned up, but readmission and relapse doesn't mean full eventual recovery is impossible.

Working on the unit for a while has opened my eyes to the ways in which an eating disorder can have a knock-on effect on every aspect of a person's life. Watching television becomes an opportunity for exercise by jiggling one's legs. Cookery programmes are watched obsessively and endless recipes noted down. Excuses are made to attempt to avoid the snack where Hula Hoops are on the menu – marketed as containing 25% extra in the packet. Things that seem petty get blown out of proportion as patients struggle for control in any way possible. The staff find affectionate terms for such incidents, like 'Cappuccino-Gate'. Chatting about certain topics can act as a trigger for some patients, so it is important to be aware of this and steer table talk away from conversational minefields.

The patients might take every opportunity to outwit a new and unwary member of staff. Offer a selection of yoghurts and the rhubarb will invariably be chosen – it's got one less calorie in it. Offer an after-dinner mint and they will be clandestinely swapped around. Patients might secrete a bottle of contraband Diet Coke in the bushes outside the hospital, persuade a visitor to smuggle in a Twix or drink copious amounts of water the night before being weighed. Listen carefully, and you might pick up the light patter of star-jumps in a locked bathroom or, after buzzing a patient out for a walk, hear the sonic boom as they accelerate into a speedy march.

The prognosis for eating disorders is good, better if it's the first instance of the illness and better still if treatment begins early. University life can be stressful and overwhelming and it is in such environments that eating disorders can develop, particularly when a person moving away from home for the first time suddenly has far more control over their diet.

In Cambridge, the University Counselling service can help and Addenbrooke's has a specialist unit for eating disorders. The illness is powerful and destructive and in serious cases sufferers find it hard to separate themselves from the eating disorder. One patient told me that they had nothing else in their life, but that doesn't have to be the case and thankfully it rarely is. Anybody with an eating disorder is, first and foremost, a person. People have ambitions, plans, ideas and a sense of humour and kindness and it is this that means that my work is never 'grim'.

4 December 2012

⇨ The above information is reprinted with kind permission from Jethro Thompson/*The Cambridge Student*. Please visit www.tcs.cam.ac.uk for further information.

A million Britons have an eating disorder – how are they treated?

It was brave of Lily Allen to admit recently that she has suffered from bulimia – and that, despite her being deeply unhappy, friends kept saying she looked great. This is a paradox about eating disorders: most sufferers aren't skeletal extremes and many patients I see with these problems look relatively healthy. But they aren't. Ultimately, if they do not get treatment, most will suffer from complications related to nutritional deficiencies, not to mention the mental distress that accompanies such obsessions.

At least one million Britons are affected by an eating disorder, according to estimates based on official diagnoses and charity surveys – but the true number could be higher, as so many of those with these illnesses never seek help. While doctors spend a large amount of time tackling those who are obese, those at the other end of the weight spectrum avoid the GP and go unnoticed – unless the problem becomes severe. It is more common for me to see a worried relative wondering how to help than a sufferer. This is the challenge of eating disorders. Similar to those battling with an addiction, it can take a long time for a sufferer to admit there is a problem and seek help.

The good news is that the prognosis for eating disorders can be very good with the right treatment and support.

Q. What is the treatment for anorexia?

Psychological treatments involve cognitive behavioural therapy, analytical therapy and group work. Severe sufferers may be hospitalised for daily therapy sessions and weight-monitoring. The physical treatment aims to slowly reintroduce a higher level of calories. This has to be done carefully to avoid electrolyte imbalances in the blood. Often people with anorexia are medicated with anti-depressants.

Q. What is the treatment for bulimia?

Treatment also aims to work on the psychological problems but needs to work on the physical problems that have arisen. Vomiting can cause severe imbalances in potassium and calcium in the body. Correcting this is vital.

Q. Do all patients with eating disorders end up on a psychiatric ward?

No. People are usually treated in a specialist eating disorders centre and this will often take the form of outpatient treatment. This can be intensive at first with regular therapy. Such centres work with all aspects of a patient's illness and professionals involved include a psychiatrist, psychologists and dieticians, as well as therapists and maybe even social workers.

Q. Can a GP treat someone with an eating disorder?

Binge eating disorder is normally managed in general practice but the other disorders are always managed by the specialist teams. The GP would certainly be a part of the team but treatment is initiated with a psychiatrist. As people stabilise, a GP can take over some of the monitoring and prescriptions. If you suspect your child has an eating disorder, talking to the GP is the first step to diagnosis.

Q. Can my GP advise me about private treatment for anorexia?

Yes. You should talk through the private treatment you are considering with your GP, who should be able to advise you on legitimate services locally.

⇨ The above information is reprinted with kind permission from Adapt Youth. Please visit www.adapteatingdistress.com for further information.

The importance of getting help

Getting help early can:

- Improve the chances of recovery. The sooner you seek help at the first signs, the sooner a young person can recover.

- Can help you feel less isolated by talking to those who can help and empower you all as a family to tackle recovery head on.

- Reduce the risks of developing life-long problems that are associated with eating disorders.

- Reduce the practical and emotional difficulties in relation to parenting a young family member with an eating disorder.

Sometimes getting help is not always easy. Many clinicians and general practitioners do not see many cases of eating disorders and so making a proper diagnosis can be difficult. If you believe or suspect your child has an eating disorder you can first of all gather evidence that makes your concerns more real.

There are still many misconceptions about eating disorders. Some myths about eating disorders are listed below.

- You have to be underweight to have an eating disorder. Most people who suffer from eating disorders are not underweight. Sufferers may feel compelled to hide their shape and weight from others by wearing baggy clothing etc.

- People who have eating disorders don't eat. Although for some not eating is an issue, most people tend to restrict or avoid certain foods such as those containing fat or higher calorie foods.

- Only girls suffer from eating disorders. Eating disorders affect boys as well. Up to one in four anorexia diagnoses in teens, are male. They are most often found in males playing sports.

- People choose to have an eating disorder. This is most definitely a myth as those suffering will tell you that they had no intention of becoming anorexic. Sufferers require much help and support from family and friends to recover and cannot do it alone.

- Eating disorders aren't very serious. Eating disorders can cause very serious medical problems. Most of these medical problems are a result of malnutrition (not getting enough nutrients) or weight-loss techniques such as vomiting.

Eating disorders must be taken seriously as they cause life long physical and emotional problems and can be fatal.

The significance of early identification and treatment

There is considerable evidence to show that the earlier treatment begins, the more successful it will be, but the first signs of an eating disorder are subtle and are often meticulously concealed by the sufferer. Parents, carers and friends may notice changes in behaviour and these should not be ignored. Parents should take their child to the GP with their concerns, who will refer you to children's specialist services. (Child and Adolescent mental health teams.)

- The above information is reprinted with kind permission from NHS Greater Glasgow and Clyde. Please visit www.nhsggc.org.uk for further information.

© NHS Greater Glasgow and Clyde 2013

Eating disorders can be beaten – tell everyone!

By Ilona Burton

It's Eating Disorders Awareness Week and the lovely people at Mind have asked me to write a blog for it. Here it is!

As my days and weeks are currently taken up with plodding along the pavements of Manchester in preparation for the London Marathon (for Mind, of course), where better to focus than on exactly that: running.

Six years ago, I was told that if I ran, I could die. Cardiac arrest and drop dead, just like that. Bizarrely, I stared into my doctor's eyes completely unfazed, left the surgery and hit the gym. I didn't care if I ended up in a heap on the floor, I didn't care about my health; I didn't care about anything at all apart from seeing the number on the scale slowly drop lower and lower and lower.

I never set myself off on a quest to be thin for the sake of fitting into size six skinny jeans or to resemble emaciated models or celebrities. If I cared what I looked like, I wouldn't have appeared zombie-like with thinning hair, terrible skin, matchstick legs and dead eyes. Trust me, it's not a good look.

No, those hours spent in a daze on the treadmill, powering up and down the swimming pool obsessively counting laps and kilometres and traipsing round the aisles of Morrison's only to leave with a few litres of diet coke and countless packs of sugar-free jelly were driven not by messages drilled into my silly, vulnerable head by evil magazines or high fashion, but by the most deadly of all mental illnesses, anorexia nervosa.

Eating disorders could be best described as all-consuming; taking over every thought, reaction, behaviour, decision; every waking moment is dictated by food and weight, and moods swing alongside the strength and power of restriction or the guilt and despair that come with the weakness of giving in to hunger – to nature. Eating disorders chip away the personality of their victims, often ruining relationships, social lives and all other avenues of enjoyment along the way. People say that eating disorders are about gaining control, but they're really about losing it in every way imaginable.

I was far from being in control. I didn't want to drag myself out of bed at 6am to sweat it out in the gym before a full day of lectures followed by Irish Dancing and more gym. I didn't want

to stare longingly at my housemate's plate as she liberally grated cheap cheddar on her spag bol. I didn't want to spend hours hopping on and off the scales, moving them around the floor of my tiny student hall cell to see if the number changed by 0.1 lb. Like it or not, my mental illness was completely and utterly, undeniably in control of me, and there it clung.

We're told in primary school that every story should have a beginning, a middle and an end. The middle section of this is of course how I got from where I was then, to where I am now, but if I told you that, we'd be here all day and this blog would be a book. Let's cut it short, for now.

Somehow, with heaps of support from friends and family, two stints in a specialised eating disorders unit, loads of time, thought, lapses, relapses, a huge amount of determination, dedication and a looming and growing fear of what the future held if I continued on that horrible, destructive path (nothing/more hospitalisations/slow death), I got to where I am now. I call it 'pretty much recovered'. Not official, but it works and I'm both happy and damn proud. I'm also proof that eating disorders can be beaten; I honestly never, ever believed that I would. How's that?!

I still have to drag myself out into the driving, icy rain to run much further than I'd like, but now it's not about burning calories or losing weight or destroying my body, it's to join an amazing team of people who all, for different reasons, wish to raise money for Mind. Everybody knows somebody with a mental illness, but without speaking out about them, sharing stories like mine or simply being aware of the facts, we'll never be able to make the changes that need to happen. Mind do a fantastic job of standing up to the stigma that still surrounds mental health, so I'm ecstatic to say that I am finally healthy and strong enough to be training for the London Marathon in support of an ongoing campaign to get people talking.

12 February 2013

⇨ The above information is reprinted with kind permission from Mind. Please visit www.mind.org.uk for further information.

To the woman who sat next to me at the eating disorders clinic

Obviously I noticed your daughter before I noticed you. I expect you are used to that. Legs so thin, how could it be any other way? I tried not to stare but it's so hard not to. People used to stare at me in much the same way, or so I've been told (I never noticed at the time). Once you'd both signed in, you came and sat next to me, with her on the other side of you. I noticed you then but only because I couldn't see her any more.

Your face didn't give away a single thing. I thought, 'if I were you, I'd cry'. I wouldn't be brave but then what do I know? Perhaps you do cry. I don't know how long you've been living with this. You must be used to it. It must take quite some time for a girl to starve herself down to the size of your daughter. You have had time to watch in horror and prepare for whatever it is that you need to prepare for. I don't know how much longer it will be like this, whether it will get worse or better, or stay the same, year in, year out. Alas, nor do you.

When I first became ill people – lots of people, doctors, nurses, relatives, anyone really – would ask me if I'd thought about what I was putting my parents through. As though somehow I'd planned it but hadn't quite considered the implications. There isn't really an answer you can give to this. Deep down, people are saying 'you're not really ill'. After all, you wouldn't tell someone with a proper illness to hurry up and recover because it was making their parents sad. And yet it is a proper illness all the same; I've seen people die of it (but wouldn't want to admit that to you). It's not a choice, nor is it a punishment reserved especially for you. Life would be much simpler if it was. We could all say sorry and then go home.

I have thought about what my illness did to my mother, in fearful, intermittent bursts. If anything, such thoughts make recovery harder, not easier. I've burned with resentment at the accusations of others, turned back in on myself, seen those who cared for me pushed far back, onto the side of those who think I'm plotting against them. There has been so much bitterness and shame. Blame is such a useless thing.

I wanted to talk to you, to tell you tell you it wasn't your fault. To tell you that now I'm a mother I almost understand just how agonising it must be for you and that I don't think 'well, why don't you just force her?' (we both know other people do). I wanted to hug you. I felt so, so bad for you. I know that doesn't mean anything, but I think you are courageous just being there with your child. Don't ever be ashamed of her or yourself. No one else can possibly know all that exists between you and all the goodness that remains.

I saw my mum this evening. We never talk about the days when we were once as you are now. Flesh or lack of it is not the thing that matters. I wish you both well.

19 March 2013

⇨ The above information is reprinted with kind permission from Glosswatch. Please visit www.glosswatch.com for further information.

© Glosswatch 2013

Mealtimes: ten ideas for supporting recovering anorexics

Parents and teachers of young people recovering from an eating disorder often find themselves in a situation where they want to offer support at meal times, but they don't know how best to help. It will depend entirely on the individual and, as long as they are well enough, you should always be guided by the young person in question, but here are ten suggestions to help you on your way.

Think about meal timings and locations

The school lunch hall or cafeteria can be a difficult place for a recovering anorexic to spend time in. You should never insist that their meals are taken there, even if it is your school's usual policy. Perhaps your school has more than one lunch sitting and the pupil would feel okay in the cafeteria at a time when their peers aren't there, or perhaps you should find somewhere different altogether, such as a classroom.

Trust them to keep their own food diary

Many recovering anorexics are expected to keep a food diary. It can be very tempting to complete this on their behalf because you know what they have eaten and are keen to ensure that it is recorded accurately. However, it can be an important show of trust to allow the pupil to complete their own food diary. Of course, if you have reason to suspect it is wildly inaccurate then consider again!

Let them eat with a friend

Having a friend or a trusted adult with them whilst they eat can make a lot of young people feel more at ease. If you arrange for this, you should ask specifically whether the friend should also be eating at the same time. Some young people will not feel comfortable eating whilst their friend is not, whilst others will want to focus on their meal but would like their friend just to talk to them, usually about something entirely non-food related if possible.

Provide specific meals

If it's practical, you can agree meals ahead with the young person and their parents and have the school provide them (or they may bring their own packed lunch). This will enable them to stick with foods they feel safe with and will also add some predictability to their meals, which can help them feel safe. Equally, you may find that if 'normal' school meals must be taken, that making the young person aware of what meal will be provided beforehand will help them to prepare themselves (though for others it will give them longer to worry, so you need to decide what is right in your situation).

Accept unusual food choices

However revolting or bizarre, if they are eating then let it pass without comment.

Let them serve themselves

Even if it is not the done thing in your school canteen, if possible let the young person serve their own food as this will help them to feel more in control of the meal. Of course, if they repeatedly serve themselves portions which are simply too small then you will have to revert to a pre-served meal. It is (unless their health provider disagrees), fine during the earlier stages of recovery for the young person to serve themselves smaller than usual portions. This can make the meal seem less daunting and they can gradually work their way up to normal servings.

Don't 'watch'

Make sure that even if you are watching them, that the young person never feels like they're being watched or spied upon. How would you like it?!

Don't talk about how much they've eaten

This can be really hard, especially if they've done really well and you want to congratulate them, but it's generally not a good idea to pass comment as 'Well done for eating half a jacket potato, that's fantastic!' can so easily be heard as 'Oh my God, I can't believe you ate so much you greedy fat pig.' If they volunteer that they are pleased with what they've eaten, a safe reply is something along the lines of 'Well done, I realise that must have been really difficult for you.'

Don't discuss food and weight concerns over lunch

If possible, steer the conversation as far away as possible from concerns about food and weight. This might be a good time to start watching soap operas to give yourself something meaningless to discuss until the meal is over!

After lunch matters too...

After they've eaten, recovering anorexics often feel really panicky, depressed or ashamed and some may try and purge themselves of the calories they've consumed, e.g. by vomiting or exercising. For these reasons it's really helpful to make sure that the young person is busy and not left alone with their feelings after lunch.

⇨ This information is based on work supported by the National Institute of Health Research under its Programme Grants for Applied Research scheme. Visit www.eatingdisordersadvice.co.uk for further support and ideas.

Anorexia patient should be force fed, High Court rules

A High Court judge has ruled that it is in the best interests of a woman who suffers from 'extremely severe' anorexia to be fed against her wishes.

Mr Justice Peter Jackson found that the 32-year-old, who has other chronic health conditions, 'lacked capacity' to make a decision about life-sustaining treatment.

Sitting at the Court of Protection in London, the judge said it was a 'very difficult decision' to make in a situation requiring 'a balance to be struck between the weight objectively to be given to life on one hand and to personal independence on the other'.

Her case had 'raised for the first time in my experience the real possibility of life-sustaining treatment not being in the best interests of a person who, while lacking capacity, is fully aware of her situation'.

Giving his conclusion in a judgement made public today, he said: 'The competing factors are, in my judgement, almost exactly in equilibrium, but having considered them as carefully as I am able, I find that the balance tips slowly but unmistakably in the direction of life-preserving treatment.

'In the end, the presumption in favour of the preservation of life is not displaced.'

He declared that 'it is lawful and in her best interests for her to be fed, forcibly if necessary'.

The 'resulting interference' with the rights of the woman, who lives in Wales and cannot be named for legal reasons, but is referred to as E, was 'proportionate and necessary in order to protect her right to life'.

The judge said of her: 'Albeit gravely unwell, she is not incurable. She does not seek death, but above all she does not want to eat or to be fed.

'She sees her life as pointless and wants to be allowed to make her own choices, realising that refusal to eat must lead to her death.'

Her case came before the court last month when an urgent application was made by her local authority, which also cannot be identified, which was 'concerned that her position should be investigated and protected'.

Mr Justice Jackson said: 'E's death was imminent. She was refusing to eat and was taking only a small amount of water.

'She was being looked after in a community hospital under a palliative care regime whose purpose was to allow her to die in comfort.'

The former medical student, described as an 'intelligent and charming person', who began to control her eating at the age of 11, has not taken solid food for more than a year and when her body mass index (BMI) was last measured it was 11.3 – a healthy BMI is in the region of 20.

E, who has also abused alcohol since adolescence as a 'means of escape', has an 'obsessive fear of weight gain'. She was 'an adult with an entrenched history of acute difficulties'.

The judge said: 'For E, the compulsion to prevent calories entering her system has become the card that trumps all others. The need not to gain weight overpowers all other thoughts.'

Explaining the reasons for his decision, the judge said: 'At its simplest, the balance to be struck places the value of E's life in one scale and the value of her personal independence in the other, with these transcendent factors being weighed in the light of the reality of her actual situation.'

He said: 'In E's situation, any decision is a heavy one. The balancing exercise is not mechanistic, but intuitive, and there are weighty factors on each side of the scales.

'On one side, I have been struck by the fact that the people who know E best do not favour further treatment.

'They think that she has had enough and believe that her wishes should be respected. They believe she should be allowed a dignified death.'

He said he acknowledged the 'impossible' position of her parents and had also reflected on what was involved in the course of treatment.

'It does not merely entail bodily intrusion of the most intimate kind, but the overbearing of E's will in a way that she experiences as abusive.'

The judge also said E's views 'are entitled to high respect'.

He added: 'She is not a child or a very young adult, but an intelligent and articulate woman, and the weight to be given to her view of life is correspondingly greater.'

Regard 'must also be had to the fact that this application was only brought after E and her family and carers had embarked a long way down the course of palliative treatment'.

He added: 'The state is now seeking to intervene very late in the day and a return to compulsion will be excruciating for them.'

The judge said he acknowledged the significant risks involved in treatment, 'not excepting a risk to life', the modest prospects of success, the 'wholesale and prolonged invasion of E's privacy and self-determination that is proposed', the 'high chance that, even if short-term progress can be made, long-term difficulties will remain' and accepted that a resumption of treatment 'deprives E of an imminent and relatively peaceful death'.

Against those 'weighty factors', the judge said he placed E's life 'in the other scale'.

He said: 'We only live once – we are born once and we die once – and the difference between life and death is the biggest difference we know.

'E is a special person, whose life is of value. She does not see it that way now, but she may in future.'

The judge went on: 'I would not overrule her wishes if further treatment was futile, but it is not. Although extremely burdensome to E, there is a possibility that it will succeed.

'Services and funding will now be provided that were not available before and it would not be right to turn down the final chance of helping this very vulnerable young woman.'

He said he was also influenced by the fact that those who know her best were not in outright opposition to treatment taking place, 'however sceptical they justifiably feel'.

The judge said: 'I record that the state, having instigated this plan of action for E in the way that it has, is now honour-bound to see it through by the provision of resources in the short, medium and long-term.

'Had the authorities not made that commitment, I would not have reached the conclusion that I have.'

15 June 2012

⇨ The above information is reprinted with kind permission from the Press Association. Please visit www.pressassociation.com for further information.

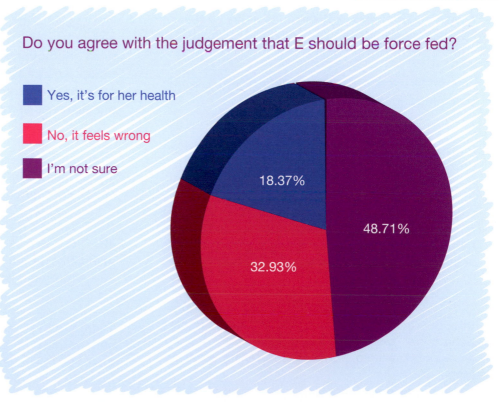

Do you agree with the judgement that E should be force fed?

- 🟦 Yes, it's for her health
- 🟥 No, it feels wrong
- 🟪 I'm not sure

18.37%

48.71%

32.93%

Key facts

⇨ Girls and women are ten times more likely than boys and men to suffer from anorexia or bulimia. (page 1)

⇨ Eating disorders usually start during the teenage years. It affects around one 15-year-old girl in every 150 and one 15-year-old boy in every 1,000. (page 1)

⇨ About four out of every 100 women suffers from bulimia at some time in their lives, rather fewer men. (page 2)

⇨ A newly released report carried out for Beat by a volunteer economist from the charity Pro Bono Economics (PBE) has found an overall estimated cost of £1.26 billion per year to the English economy from eating disorders – and could be much higher. (page 9)

⇨ 95 per cent of people who diet will return to their usual weight, or weigh even more, within two years. (page 10)

⇨ Recent research shows that not only are females who have Type 1 diabetes at twice the risk of developing anorexia or bulimia, as many as 40% of 15- to 30-year-olds regularly omit insulin. (page 11)

⇨ One in 14 women have an eating disorder during pregnancy. (page 12)

⇨ Almost 50% of people with eating disorders meet the criteria for depression. (page 15)

⇨ Only one in ten men and women with eating disorders receive treatment. Only 35% of people that receive treatment for eating disorders get treatment at a specialised facility for eating disorders. (page 15)

⇨ Over one-half of teenage girls and nearly one-third of teenage boys use unhealthy weight control behaviours such as skipping meals, fasting, smoking cigarettes, vomiting and taking laxatives. (page 15)

⇨ In a survey of 185 female students on a college campus, 58% felt pressure to be a certain weight, and of the 83% that dieted for weight loss, 44% were of normal weight. (page 15)

⇨ 20% of people suffering from anorexia will prematurely die from complications related to their eating disorder, including suicide and heart problems. (page 16)

⇨ It's often assumed that anorexia is fuelled by vanity and a desire to emulate skinny celebrities. In reality, eating disorders, including anorexia, are serious mental health problems, triggered by a complex interplay of low self-worth, difficulties in coping with problems and – possibly – genetics. (page 20)

⇨ Eating disorder statistics from Beat found that 1% of children felt they could talk to their parents about their eating-related concerns, 9% of children felt they might be able to talk to someone at school, 17% of children felt they might be able to talk to a doctor or nurse and 92% of children felt they couldn't tell anyone. (page 21)

⇨ Statistics show that nearly 600 children under the age of 13 were treated in hospital in England, including 197 aged between five and nine, after developing eating disorders. (page 22)

⇨ The results showed that adolescents – both boys and girls – who had looked at gossip magazines most often during a study, were also most likely to report worrying changes in eating behaviours. In contrast, exposure to television or to other types of magazines appeared to have no effect. (page 28)

⇨ Over 50% of those surveyed said that Facebook makes them more self-conscious about their bodies and their weight. (page 29)

⇨ 40% of men said they had posted negative comments about their own bodies, compared to 20% of women. (page 29)

⇨ There are over 500 pro-ana and pro-mia websites and the latest studies predict that they attract more than 500,000 unique visitors a year of which the majority are teenage girls and one in five are aged between six and 11. (page 30)

Glossary

Anorexia athletica

An eating disorder and mental health condition that involves excessively exercising in order to lose weight.

Anorexia nervosa

An eating disorder and mental health condition that involves an immoderate restriction on food intake.

Binge eating disorder

An eating disorder where a person feels compelled to consume large quantities of food in a short period of time, often when they are not hungry.

Body dysmorphic disorder

A mental health condition where a person has an excessive concern over their body image and what they perceive as their 'flaws'.

Bulimia nervosa

An eating disorder and mental health condition that involves excessive food consumption followed by actions such as vomiting or the use of laxatives to compensate for their food intake.

Diabulimia

An eating disorder in which people with Type 1 diabetes deliberately give themselves less insulin than they need in order to lose weight.

Disordered eating

A term used to describe eating habits that can be considered 'irregular' but do not warrant diagnosis as anorexia or bulimia nervosa.

Eating disorder

A term used to describe a range of psychological disorders that involve disturbed eating habits such as anorexia or bulimia nervosa.

Faddy eating

Similar to fussy eating; often involves the exclusion or avoidance of certain foods for no discernible reason.

Gluten

A protein that is found in foods processed from wheat and other grains.

Intervention

The process of getting someone to seek professional help for the treatment of a disorder, condition or addiction.

Orthorexia nervosa

An eating disorder and mental health condition characterised by an extreme avoidance of food that the sufferer considers to be unhealthy.

Pica

A disorder that involves the consumption of non-nutritive substances such as dirt, hair or sand.

Pro-ana

The promotion of eating disorders such as anorexia nervosa as a lifestyle choice.

Thinspiration

Images or videos of women that are slim or of an unhealthy weight as an 'inspiration' for weight-loss or for the promotion of eating disorders.

Assignments

1. Read the article on page one *Eating disorders: information and advice*. Create an information booklet, based on this article, that will be made available in your school and your local GP's office. You should include an introduction to Eating Disorders, signs of having an eating disorder and some helplines, websites and organisations that people might visit for guidance.

2. Read the article on page four *Facts and figures*. At the end of the article there is a web-link that provides information about Pica. Visit this site and make some notes, then find a family member or friend who has never heard of the disorder and use your notes to explain it to them.

3. In pairs, discuss the following questions: What is disordered eating? How does it relate to eating disorders?

4. In small groups, create a presentation about the risks of disordered eating that would be suitable for a school assembly. You should explain the problems surrounding disordered eating and make sure that you include a section on healthy eating habits. You could also produce handouts.

5. Create a questionnaire for young people who are worried that they might have an eating disorder. To take this further, think about how you might turn your questionnaire into an app. What would you call your app? What would the logo be? Would you include helpline numbers at the end? Design your app.

6. Using the articles in this book, and on the Internet, research diabulimia and write an article for your local paper or magazine exploring this disorder.

7. Use the article on page 13 *What health professionals should know about eating disorders* to produce a guide for health professionals to consult when dealing with young people who have eating disorders. Your guide could be a webpage, a poster, a leaflet or simply a letter.

8. Read the article *The many consequences of anorexia nervosa* on page 14. In pairs, discuss your daily routines and think about what challenges you would have to overcome if you were struggling with an eating disorder. Make some notes and feedback your ideas to the rest of the class.

9. In the article on page four, the organisation Beat notes that there is a severe lack of UK-based statistics exploring the prevalence of eating disorders. The statistical information on pages 15 and 16 is taken, in the most part, from US-based studies. Using this as a starting point, make a list of the information that you think should be available in the UK and where you think it should come from i.e. GPs, NHS hospitals, Private clinics etc.

10. Imagine that you are an Agony Aunt/Uncle who has received a letter from the parent of a thirteen-year-old. This parent is worried that their son/daughter has an eating disorder. Write a reply to them, giving advice on how to handle the situation.

11. Using the information from this book, discuss with a partner the possible triggers for eating disorders. Make a list and then consider whether there are different triggers for men and women. Discuss your answers with the rest of your class.

12. Do you think that size zero models should be used in magazines and advertising? Stage a debate in which one half of the class argues that they should be used, and the other half argues that they should not be used.

13. Write a letter to your local MP arguing that pro-ana sites should be banned. Make sure that you explain the reasons for your argument.

14. Read the book *Massive* by Julia Bell. Write a review of the book, exploring how well you think the author deals with the topic of eating disorders and whether you think the characters' struggles are realistic.

15. Research the musical figure Karen Carpenter, who tragically died after a long struggle with the eating disorder anorexia. Write a blog post exploring Karen's life and the consequences of her disorder.

16. Choose an illustration from this book and explore what you think the artist was trying to portray in their cartoon. Do you think they have achieved this? What might you change about the illustration if you could?

Acknowledgements

While every care has been taken to trace and acknowledge copyright, the publisher tenders its apology for any accidental infringement or where copyright has proved untraceable.

Illustrations:

Pages 9 & 23: Don Hatcher; pages 14 & 25: Simon Kneebone; pages 19 & 28: Angelo Madrid.

Images:

All images are sourced from iStock, Morguefile or SXC, except where specifically acknowledged otherwise.

Additional acknowledgements:

Editorial on behalf of Independence Educational Publishers by Cara Acred.

With thanks to the Independence team: Mary Chapman, Sandra Dennis, Christina Hughes, Jackie Staines and Jan Sunderland.

Cara Acred

Cambridge

September 2013